Sweet Freedom

*Mending a Heart Broken by
Mental Illness*

By

Bonnie Twomey

Sweet Freedom: Mending a Heart Broken by Mental Illness, Published October, 2020

Editorial and proofreading services: Kathleen A. Tracy, Karen Grennan
Interior layout and cover design: Howard Johnson

Photo Credits: Author photo Courtesy of Mike Indi

 **SDP Publishing**

Published by SDP Publishing, an imprint of SDP Publishing Solutions, LLC.

The stories in this book reflect the author's recollection of events. Some names, locations, and identifying characteristics have been changed to protect the privacy of those depicted. Dialogue has been re-created from memory.

To obtain permission(s) to use material from this work, please submit a written request to:

SDP Publishing
Permissions Department
PO Box 26, East Bridgewater, MA 02333
or email your request to info@SDPPublishing.com.

ISBN-13 (print): 978-1-7356973-3-8
ISBN-13 (ebook): 978-1-7356973-4-5

Library of Congress Control Number: 2020918539

Printed in the United States of America

*In loving memory of my father,
Jack, and my mother, Peggy.*

2020

Lucia,

Thank you
for your
friendship
through
all these
years

Love,
Bonnie

TABLE OF CONTENTS

Acknowledgments

Great thanks to Lisa Akoury-Ross, my publisher; Kathleen Tracy, my editor; Jack Churchill, the producer of The Bonnie Tapes; *Lucia Miller, LeRoy Spaniol, and Carol Goldman, my cheerleader.*

Prologue

I woke from a deep sleep to morning sunshine filtering through the sheer, white curtains. Recently fallen snow muted the *whoosh* of traffic from Interstate 95 visible across the street outside my bedroom window. Shaking the lingering grogginess out, I headed to the kitchen, made a pot of coffee, and drank it while sitting at the same kitchen table my dad and his family had used as children. Then I read spiritual passages from a book given to me as a present more than ten years earlier. Starting the day through my faith in prayer is a part of my daily routine that I depend on. I put my life in God's hands, trusting His goodness for happiness and contentment.

I know that when I appreciate my life, I'm doing the best I can and doing exactly what I need, want, and expect of myself. It's been a long journey to become a better person and Christian and to gain a sense of compassion and caring for people, something far more powerful than whatever challenged me. And it all began at 9 Sunset Avenue.

CHAPTER

1

I WAS BORN SEPTEMBER 16, 1964, at Saint Margaret's Hospital in Boston. At the time it was the largest maternity hospital in the United States. It shared its campus with St. Mary's, a shelter for unwed mothers, many of whom gave up their infants for adoption. I believe that was something my older sister, Layla, probably wished our mother had done with me.

She was never happy that I came home and regularly told me, "If I wasn't born, you wouldn't be here." Then she would roll me up in blankets, a sort of torture.

As a toddler my hips were turned inward, so I wore foot braces—two custom-made shoes held together by a metal bar—to bed every night. The idea was that forcing my feet to stay in one position and bit-by-bit turning them completely outward by applying pressure would correct my ill-placed hips. Layla took me out of my crib one night because I was crying in pain. She felt so bad for me that she took the braces off. I remember my mother, Peggy, begging my dad to let me have surgery. He refused.

But my dad found a use for me and exposed me to the realities of politics and life at a young age. When I was no more than four years old, I walked up countless stairs to ring doorbells and ask strangers to vote for him. With a winning smile and innocent, big, blue eyes, I was a sure bet. I didn't want to campaign, but my dad told me how well I was doing and that the people I talked to loved me, so I continued. I never understood why he hated me so much if strangers seemed willing to accept me. And as I got older, I became increasingly aware of his insecurity and negativity, which he directed at me.

Growing up in my family was both exciting and difficult. We were generally held in high esteem by our friends and my dad's political supporters, but he also had enemies. When he was running for the state senate, there were people who took down his political signs from local residents' front yards. I was confused, unsure who to trust because I never knew who did those awful things to us. One night when Layla and I were very young, my father told my mother and us to stand by the front door and be quiet. He armed himself with a rifle, and we stood with him until he said it was okay to go to bed.

While my dad was running for the senate, we had our family portrait taken for the *Medford Daily Mercury*. I was proud to be dressed in my favorite outfit and wanted to look beautiful, but Layla told me I was ugly. Her insult also made me afraid that I'd look terrible in the photograph, and everyone would think poorly of me. But I had to suppress my disappointment, anger, and fears because I'd been taught to always be gracious in public and never complain.

That often held true at home, too. My dad said dinner time was the best time of the day, and he wanted to enjoy being with his family. So, my sister and I were forbidden to talk about how we felt, share any problems, or even express our opinions. We could only talk superficially about what we did that day and were expected to keep our emotions hidden. Essentially it was a form of children being seen and not heard.

Layla and my best friends growing up were Eddie and Christie, who lived on the next block. Their parents, Colleen and Henry, partied with my mom and dad just about every weekend. Everyone in the neighborhood was invited. They shared laughter, drank alcohol, and played music so loudly it could be heard three blocks away.

My dad hung a wooden plaque on our kitchen wall that read: *Support the two-party system. One party a week is not enough.* Above our living room fireplace hung a large eagle holding the American flag.

Colleen kept some vodka and orange juice in her refrigerator. Not knowing it was spiked, Eddie drank a glass before going to school. Well, he got drunk and fell asleep during class.

When his elementary school teacher asked, "What's the matter with you?" he answered, "Oh, the Twomey's had another one of their parties."

Colleen told this story to me years later when I was in college. We laugh about it even now. Today, even a respected name living in an upscale community would be thoroughly questioned if their child came to school buzzed. But back then it was uncommon for any authority figure to question our integrity. Having top lawyers and powerful law enforcement professionals in my immediate family, we felt we could get away with everything.

Our neighborhood was close-knit, and every summer we'd have a block party on one of the dead-end streets. My uncle was Medford's chief of police, so we had no worries of getting into trouble. A lot of food and alcohol was consumed, and many games played. One summer my dad rented out the Tufts University track and field gymnasium, where the other kids and I competed in long-distance track and sprint competitions.

Layla, Christie, and I took all sorts of dance lessons together. We learned to Irish dance and took part in the Irish Fest. Attending Gloria's School of Acting I was taught how to sit, hold my hands, eat, and many more lessons on how to be perfect and gracious in public. Lilly, my best girlfriend in grammar school, and I took gymnastic lessons together. At home we climbed trees and shouted aloud to the world that we had a crush on Jake, the lead singer for a local band called Finding Time. We had met him through my dad's friend Andy, who was a band manager and had booked Frank Sinatra a few gigs in his singing career. Jake and his band came to our house and signed our autograph books. Later my sister, her friends, Lilly, and I went to his outdoor concerts. I complained that I smelled something awful. Layla told me to shut up—it was pot!

On most weekends my other friends and I played street games and thought it was fun to cause trouble, like stealing shopping carts from a local grocery store. We raced them around the block, one kid in the cart, another pushing it. Once in a while, we would play dodgeball in the Medford High School gymnasium. For a while on weekends, we would have boy-girl parties at someone's home and play 45s. But after a while the girls got bored and started bullying each other. They were young but already knew how to fight.

My dad openly disapproved of me hanging around with this crowd, who lived on the west side of the city. This was the area where his political signs were vandalized. He called it a rough part of town and told me they would not treat me well. He gave me an ultimatum, but nothing came of it. And he was wrong; my friends treated me fine. I never had any disagreements or problems with them.

That same year my athletic ability began to surface, and I played shortstop on my church softball team, the Sacred Heart Streakers, which my dad coached. I felt like I fit in and loved to play the game. But when we won the league championship,

I realized that other people noticed me, and I hated to be in the limelight. It reminded me of my father's political life and the consequences of living in the public eye. If you did something good, people would do anything for you; however, if you failed them, they could destroy your reputation. I was unhappy, knowing that if I allowed people to make me feel proud of myself for succeeding, that also meant they could hurt me and turn their back on me. I knew what it felt like to be disappointed in someone, and I didn't want anyone to feel disappointed in me.

My fondest childhood memories are of the summers and weekends I spent vacationing in West Yarmouth on Cape Cod. After my softball championship I never forgot our first summer at Silver Leaf Lane. After taking a sickle to the backyard and painting the house colonial red, my mom, Layla, and I enjoyed our new summer home. My dad worked in Boston during the week and drove out to the Cape on weekends.

While there my mom introduced me to the library, and I was instantly hooked. I discovered Nancy Drew and devoured just about the entire series. We'd sun ourselves on plastic lounge chairs in the backyard and read all day. I felt such a wonderful connection and developed a bond with her that never broke.

When our family took a trip to the Cape for a weekend, several of our friends would pull into our driveway on their bicycles before we could even get out of the car and unpack. It was always so great to see them. They made me feel special. I enjoyed their company, and they returned their friendship through kindness and common interests. I never felt judged and always felt comfortable being myself, and happy knowing that I was liked for who I was, not being judged as a part of a political family.

We were part of the Englewood Beach crowd, and we all learned how to sail fourteen foot O'Jays and Sunfish sailboats—rag bags. We sped through the harbor in the boys' motorboats—stink pots—or would sun ourselves on a houseboat. When two brothers, Jay and Donny, sped by my girlfriends and me while water skiing, they would blare: *Today is your birthday* and pull mooners. We held beach parties that lasted all night, drank beer, and listened to the Beatles and the Rolling Stones.

CHAPTER

2

AS TIME WENT BY, my circle of best friends in Medford changed. I drifted away from Eddie and Christie. Lilly attended a junior high school on the west side of town. My sister was a year ahead of me at the Lincoln Junior High School, and she made new friends too. This made me feel alone and unsettled.

Layla and I ended up dating two best friends, who were both popular and cute. Randy dated my sister, and Peter was my boyfriend. They would come to our house on their dirt bikes. My mom loved them, but a lot of her friends told her to keep them away from us because they were bad news. There was a rumor that someone had been found dead in the trunk of Peter's father's car.

I found a new object of my affection and decided to break up with Pete. But when he beat me to it and dumped me first, for some reason my heart was broken. Layla kept dating Randy for a while but they eventually both moved on.

In eighth grade I began to hang around with my sister's friends at her high school. I was only thirteen but felt like I fit in. They were cool and smoked weed—something I could never do with friends in my school. We were called *the girls* and all wore matching long jean jackets, and at times we all wore blue satin coats with matching hats. Together with *the boys* we were *the gang*.

Eventually my eighth-grade girlfriends kicked me out of their little clique because I was hanging out with the older kids after school. I was walking to school with Kristie, Carla, and Stephanie. They walked far ahead then turned and said I couldn't hang around them. They accused me of using them because after school I was hanging out with other kids. I wasn't using them. I simply had a lot of friends from two different schools. I thought *Lucky me*.

I began dreading going to school. I felt alone and hated. Tormented. At lunch I would watch my old friends eat together, laugh, and have a good time. On weekends they all hung out at the same park. My family and I spent most of our weekends at West Yarmouth. There was nothing I wanted more than to fit in again but being away so much made it difficult to bond with anyone at school. The rejection led to a depression that lasted for a good year and a half. Even when it lifted, I never quite forgave them for abandoning me. I had a lot of confusion I needed to work out, especially regarding relationships.

I made new junior high friends in Medford, Billy and Lisa, who both liked to party. Lisa had introduced me to Billy because he wanted to date me. I thought he was cute, so we went steady. The three of us spent most of our free time together. Sometimes they included their mutual friends from the previous year. I also met some of Billy's friends, but the relationships never quite bonded.

One day Billy came alone to the Platte School where my high school friends hung out, which was very surprising because he was uninvited. One of the boys punched him out before he got to the steps. Staying with the tough crowd seemed to be my only option. There was a part of me that felt like I fit in with the burnouts. I began to smoke pot and abuse alcohol every day. I hated what I was doing to my dad's reputation, but I didn't think a thirteen-year-old could do that much damage.

My math teacher would listen to WCOZ with Lisa and me. It was a popular rock radio station out of Medford that gave anyone permission to smoke pot after noon—sort of like happy hour but with cannabis instead of alcohol. I got high every morning before school and every afternoon after school. I couldn't imagine life without it. It was part of my lifestyle.

Lisa would take her parents' valium and we would drink their alcohol. We smoked opium, Columbian gold, and Panama Red. Vodka knocked me out, but beers with a couple of joints were just fine. There were times our pot was laced with other drugs. We knew it was bad, but we would smoke it anyway. I was having fun most of the time but found myself feeling more dependent on pot.

One afternoon while partying after school with Billy, he wanted to have sex without the door closed even though his friends were in the other room. When I refused, he made me feel like an awful person. His friends looked down on me because I couldn't handle the drugs—the valium and alcohol were too much—and it embarrassed Billy.

My parents always went out on weekends to party with their friends, so on one of those nights my sister Layla, Lisa, Billy and I got together. Lisa wanted to get a dime bag, so Billy brought us to some dealers, bought the pot, and then we went back to my house where we sat around listening to tunes and getting high, keeping Billy busy rolling the joints. All of a sudden we laughed in hysterics and were out of control the entire night.

The next day Lisa and I smoked more before going to Sunday church. Monday during school lunch we smoked again in the girl's bathroom. It was raining so the gym class had to stay inside and play volleyball. I can remember walking onto the court and seeing the ball flying toward me in slow motion, I stood there, and a girl in my class, Donna, hit it away. Then I blacked out. The next thing I remember is walking down the corridor and into my class.

Everyone looked at me, and a girl named Kristine—loudly—said, "What the hell are you on?"

I swayed down the aisle to my seat then blacked out for several days. I was never sure why the drugs had such a damaging effect on me; maybe I overdosed.

For a while my athletic ability had continued to develop. I had a talent for running and was breaking all sorts of athletic records. I was a good skier taking the expert trails from the summit. But then partying became more important than training.

One day my physical education teacher asked me to run with a student from Medford High School to pace my time. Afterward my teacher told me my time was too slow, my running no doubt impaired from smoking cigarettes. I was so disappointed in the results and in myself. My first chance of being successful was destroyed, and I knew I was responsible. But it did little to change my behavior.

I spent most of my school days at Lincoln Junior High School causing trouble with other friends I made. We would pull pranks and go to class stoned even when the teacher was giving lessons. We would laugh the entire day. Home economics was purely an hour of fun and mayhem. I would throw eggs in the washing machine. I would heat up a large spoon from a stove burner and chase my friend Scott out of the classroom and around the gym, laughing hysterically. The teacher never punished me, so I felt as if I could get away with any sort of bad behavior.

I was on the school council and went on a weekend trip to Washington, DC. We spent the night in a hotel. Our teachers went out for a few hours, so I decided to have some fun and be wild. I walked on the outside of the ledge of our bedroom window to the next room. I had to be eight stories above the parking lot. The next morning we teased the teachers about them having bad hangovers after going out on the town, and they never found out what we had done the night before.

Toward the end of the school year I was put on in-school suspension for excessive tardiness and missing first class. Instead of being sent home for the rest of the year, I sat in the back of a classroom every day. Kids and teachers would come and go, but I stayed in the back and raised hell. It was the best time I had all year.

CHAPTER

3

I WAS STILL IN GRADE SCHOOL WHEN I MET CARL.
Our parents were friends and they would go camping together
at Sebago Lake in Maine. Carl's sister Maureen would look
after us in their home in Medford.

Several years later Carl and his parents moved to
Portland, Maine. His parents invited my family to camp with
them at Sebago Lake for about a week. At night we escaped the
doldrums of our parents' company by joining local teenagers
at bonfires. They smoked pot, as did Layla and Carl, but the
joint always passed me by because I was too young.

Carl and I developed a long-distance relationship and
kept in touch mostly by mail. I loved to open his letters. He
would always make me laugh by saying things that were so
intelligently stupid. He was a walking encyclopedia of history.
I admired him for his intelligence.

The first time I met Carl's sister Maureen was when she
watched us while our parents were away for the weekend. I
liked her. I thought she was cool. A few years later I discovered she had great pot and learned that at one point in her
life she'd been hooked on heroin. I remember staying with
Maureen at her apartment one night in Medford. Carl was
visiting her, and their parents invited me to stay with them
and went away for the weekend. I got so stoned I felt as though

I was melting into the wall behind me. Carl blared tunes, and we watched TV with the volume off. It was so easy to get lost in the high.

Carl and I developed a great friendship. He made me laugh. I felt a bond between us, something special even though when we were in high school, he lived in Maine, and I lived in Medford. Both Carl and I were causing all sorts of trouble. We would skip school and do all sorts of dangerous drugs. We both had to wear a uniform during our freshman year of high school. After school I wore low-cut shirts and Levi's, and Carl wore T-shirts and jeans. Once in a while he would wear a worn-out old cowboy hat. I thought he was great.

We remained close friends through our college years and beyond. I was attracted to his kindness and compassion. I visited him in Maine for weekends or sometimes a week at a time. He made me feel so comfortable. His mom read tarot cards for me, I met his friends, and we all had fun when we were together. I loved to visit him.

He had wanted to date me, but I had no interest in him as a boyfriend, so our relationship never went beyond friendship. That was very difficult for Carl; he could never understand why I didn't love him romantically. At times he put distance between us, but then he would call, and I always let him back in to my life.

My dad's friend Andy knew many famous or prominent people, including Dick Goodwin, who had been President John F. Kennedy's political advisor. When I was in grammar school, Layla and I stayed overnight at one of their homes, somewhere near Harvard, Massachusetts, and slept in the workers' quarters located in an apple orchard. We had a babysitter who watched us overnight. I got up the next morning before my parents and Andy and his wife got back to the house. I knew they had been partying all night because they seemed strung out.

During the time I was in junior high, Layla, Lisa, and I stayed at one of the Goodwin estates in Concord, Massachusetts. The house had fourteen bedrooms, all with adjacent bathrooms, and a spiraling, marble staircase. The backyard, which was surrounded by woods, had a patio that led to a pool. After getting high on weed in the morning, we swam in the pool and continued to party at night.

Two elderly women were living there but other than making a continental breakfast, they kept their distance from us although one of the women miraculously found the orthodontic retainer I had lost. We explored the home and found a huge stash of pot on an end table in one of the bedrooms, obviously not hidden well. I wanted to sneak some, but we left it alone because we did not want to get caught.

My family and I stayed at other Goodwin estates as well. We would go to shooting practice in their yard and ski at Sugerloaf, a resort in Western Maine. While exploring the attic in their barn house we found a huge stash of toys that belonged to one of his kids. Among the toys were handwritten letters from the former First Lady Jackie Kennedy to Dick. It was a gold mine.

One night during the same visit, a professional football player with the New England Patriots showed up with several cases of beer and everyone was openly smoking weed. Mom was angry that they were being so indiscreet in front of her children.

My sister, Andy's brother-in-law, and I were stoned too, but the adults did not know. After my parents and their friends went out, we blared the Moody Blues from the turntable, got high, and lit a raging fire in the fireplace. It was so large we threw in a large, wooden stump used as a chair. They never noticed the chair was gone.

My father once accidently fired an elephant gun he had found in their barn and put a hole in a wooden canoe stored there. The gun had such a strong kickback it hit my dad's upper nose and he needed a butterfly stitch. Dick later told Andy someone must have broken into the barn and shot a hole in the boat. My dad never owned up to it, worried Dick could ruin his career through his connections.

4

THE SUMMER BEFORE I ENTERED THE NINTH GRADE
my dad decided to run for Middlesex County treasurer, his
first major campaign; all of his previous races were local. My
family campaigned morning, noon, and night. We passed out
flyers, worked in the campaign headquarters, and held signs in
subways at six o'clock in the morning. We never complained.
After all, it was for my dad. My mom was his campaign manager. She worked so hard to do everything right. I was too
young to be more involved in her work.

That same summer, a sixteen-year-old transfer student
from Stockholm lived with us, a tall, brunette named Hillivive.
We called her Levi and loved her. She campaigned for my dad,
and the mayor of Medford presented her with a key to the city.

Even though she barely knew English, I was able to communicate with her, and learning about life in Sweden opened
my mind and my world. We would curl each other's hair and
talk about life in our home countries. She taught us about
her customs, and we taught her how to smoke pot and not
get caught. We brought Levi to the Cape house, and she met
all of our friends. It was the best summer I'd ever had up to
that time.

The last night she spent with us at the Cape, Layla, Levi,
and I were arm-in-arm and sang: *Hey, hey, we're the Monkees.*

Levi broke down in tears. She was having the best time in her life and did not want to leave. After she flew back to Sweden we kept in touch by mail for a while but then eventually lost communication.

After Levi left and a new school year started, the bad news came: my dad lost the election. My family, his friends, and political supporters were devastated. My parents were exhausted and went away for the weekend, leaving Layla and I with the house to ourselves. That was when I confided in her that I was very unhappy, depressed, and confused about my immediate future and thought I might go crazy.

When my parents came home, she told them I needed help, but they said they would deal with whatever was bothering me later. I felt a distance from her. I was never sure why but I had a feeling it was because of how my parents disregarded her concerns and her asking them to take care of my needs. We continued our friendship, and she often included me in nights out with her friends. I felt comfortable with her and loved and valued her presence in my life.

There was no question in my dad's mind that I should join Layla and go to Arlington Catholic High School. That meant I had to leave all my old friends who were going to attend Medford High. I wanted to hang out with kids who did not do drugs and who enjoyed playing sports. I wanted to change my life and become a better person with potential. But I never told my parents, mainly because problems in my parents' marriage were causing our family life to deteriorate and there was so much tension at home.

I made new friends in Arlington and we'd go ice-skating. I also loved going to the class dances and joined the track team. My new friends were great, and I always had a good time when we went out on a Saturday night. The two girls who sat behind me in homeroom invited me to take art lessons with them. My teacher, Laura, was tough and never let anyone leave with a bad painting. I continued to paint and a few years later joined the Winchester Art Association. There was an award show, and I won the Most Popular painting ribbon. The *Medford Daily Mercury* published an article about my success along with a picture of me standing beside my artwork. My dad was proud of me and encouraged me to pursue an art career.

But a couple months into my freshman year I fell into a serious depression that felt physically heavy, like I had the world on my shoulders. I wanted to be happy, but I never smiled, or cracked any jokes, and I quit the track team. No one seemed to notice my malaise, so I suffered needlessly.

The nuns let me know what they thought of me—they didn't like me—and that I belonged at Medford High School. It was such a put down. Staying at my new school seemed impossible. I missed the bus almost every morning. I would walk into the school, and not let the school's administrator know I was there. If the nuns gave me shit, I gave it back, end of story. They insulted me in the classroom in front of the other students. I felt like an awful person.

The nuns could not get away with calling me Daisy. I would say, "That is not my name," then turn on my heel and walk away because I was annoyed at the insult.

Near the end of the school year I found a letter mailed to my parents from the Arlington Catholic Admissions Department. I was afraid they might say negative things about me, and I didn't want my parents to read it. So even though I knew I shouldn't have, I opened it. They told my parents they did not want me to return the next year unless I brought my grades up.

I panicked. I didn't know how my mother knew about the contents of the letter, but she approached me on the subject. She asked where I would like to go to school. It was then that

I felt my dreams and my life were in shambles. I felt a deep sense of dread because a year passed, and I didn't know how to go into sophomore year and make new friends.

After I left Arlington Catholic I somehow thought I finally had the chance to go to a school that offered a curriculum I might be more interested in, like acting and self-defense classes. I imagined what this type of school would be like but wasn't sure where to find it—or if it even existed. My dad arranged to have me take an entrance exam to attend other high schools that were private but not parochial. I wasn't sure where.

The day I went to take an entrance test, my dad told me he had found pot in my drawer, so I asked him for permission to smoke cigarettes. He said yes. Even so, I was shaken up and could not concentrate. When I got the scores back, they were too low. My dad told me to act like it never happened and let finding the pot go. I felt so ashamed. I thought my dad had given up on me and would never respect me again or have any hope for my future. I needed my parents now more than any other time. I should have studied harder, stopped doing drugs and getting drunk.

I did not want to go to college because I hated school too much. It always made me anxious. I needed help finding direction in my life. I didn't have anywhere to turn, not even to my family. It would not have felt natural. My dad was visibly upset when I enrolled at Medford High School as a sophomore and told him I wanted to take a business curriculum. I felt a separation from my dad knowing he didn't care in the ways I needed him to. I was afraid to go to him for advice, but I desperately needed direction in my life.

I became increasingly depressed and I wasn't happy with anything. My life completely changed going to Medford High School. I felt tremendous guilt and continued to turn to drugs because I thought that was my only option. I felt I had lost the chance to know anyone who was athletic or liked to ski, work in an art studio, or sail. The high school had so many kids

I didn't know where to find anyone I felt suitable to connect with. I didn't know taking a college curriculum would have given me a better chance.

As my sister Layla and I got older, we developed different lifestyles, went to different schools, and had different interests. For a short while in our early teens we had shared the same friends, and in high school we double-dated a lot. But then our circle of friends continued to change, and we spent less time together.

I hung out with people who had a history of drug abuse. It seemed everyone I met got high. I felt like I could not—or did not want to—relate to anyone who did not. To me they were dull, not cool. People who did drugs seemed exciting, living life on the edge. I never had to buy my own drugs. My friends dealt and always gave them to me for free.

Our parents were angry because Carl and I did not take our high school education seriously and would party together when I would visit him in Maine. The best times I had with Carl were when we were drunk and stoned. His friends were cute, and they liked me a lot, so I felt comfortable hanging around with everyone at the bonfires and at parties.

At Medford High I met all kinds of people. I dated and developed friendships. Even though I knew many of the students, I felt alone and lost because I felt I had no future. The school had more than a thousand kids, and the administration had security guards to combat drugs and racial violence, but there were too many of us to teach. I hated the yellow and orange walls in the halls covered with graffiti.

When my family and I spent time vacationing at the Cape house I would run wild. There were times I would not go home for a few days. When I finally did, it was to calm my parents' worry. My girlfriends would let me sleep at their homes, and I would borrow their clothes. My friends and I were too young to have a driver's license, so to get around we would hitchhike. Plenty of times we'd party with whoever we got a ride from. My best girlfriend would hitchhike to other states. She was beautiful and vulnerable, and I thought she was too much of a risk-taker. I worried about her, but not as much as she worried about me.

My first serious boyfriend was Bob who lived in West Yarmouth. He was in the foster care system, but I loved him very much. One visit to the Cape when I was grounded, he came to the window of my bedroom. I jumped out, and we spent the night at the beach. My parents were furious and worried as hell. Andy and his wife Katie were there, having dinner with my parents. They jumped in their car and searched everywhere and eventually caught us walking back to my house. They let it go and did not punish me. They actually asked me to join them. Something I really didn't want to do so I told them no.

All in all I was extremely unhappy. I struggled to be a good person. I felt alone and responsible for my own future but did not know how to make the changes. I had no caring and support that should have come from my parents. They didn't know what to do, so they neglected me. Let me go.

I held onto some values to be a better person and participated in sports with my family and with my friends at the Cape. I had both. On one hand I lived a healthy lifestyle, and on the other hand I abused drugs and alcohol. There were many times I wanted something different, something better from my life. In the morning on the way to school, the city bus would pass a security guardhouse and drive up a hill to the courtyards. It felt like going into a jail. There were drug dealers pushing drugs, anything you could imagine. They called it the C wall.

I always felt empty inside when I passed by the C wall. I never wanted to get high before eight in the morning.

Sometimes I did, and by the time the eight o'clock bell rang to go inside the building to homeroom class I was always too stoned to concentrate on my classwork. At lunchtime there were at least a hundred kids in the courtyards. Most of the students I knew got high on marijuana during lunchtime. I felt it was wrong because it would ruin the whole day of classes. Even so, at times I would make the mistake and get high. It was a bad choice because then I'd skip the next class, unable to concentrate on the subject material, or just leave school.

My school was known for racial violence. There were fistfights, bad ones. There was an unwritten law that no white girl could go into the black girl's bathroom. You did this only if you wanted to get knifed or beat up.

I hung out with different groups of people, mostly from Morrison Park and the kids from the Dame School. I grew up with the gang that hung out at the school. I knew them from the neighborhood where I grew up in Medford. I would have them at my parents' home every day after school to listen to albums and get stoned.

One afternoon during the wintertime of my sophomore year, one of my father's clients named Frank dropped by the house to give my dad legal forms. Frank's sister was one of my friends. He'd been hit on his motorcycle, had survived grotesque injuries, and was now getting a settlement. He was twenty-one years old and I was sixteen. When Frank came by the house again, he asked me if I would like to get high. Layla came home and was completely pissed at me because I was too stoned to move. When I decided to sleep it off, I told Frank I needed to make beef stew for the family dinner. He had an odd response. He laughed and told me he would make it.

And he did. But when my mother looked at it, she said, "Who made this?"

∽

During the second semester of my sophomore year I met Cindy, Suzanne, and Gale. Cindy introduced me to people at Morrison Park, which was a drug store—literally. Kids would pull up in cars, a dealer would approach, and a transaction would follow. Then we would hang out and get high. We would all clear out by 8:00 p.m. and go someplace else to avoid the risk of getting busted.

I knew Frank at the same time I was hanging at Morrison Park. Through him I fell in with the toughest crowd in the city, even though I was too young for this group. Frank and I continued to do a lot of drugs together. I didn't know what I was getting myself into. In the beginning I didn't realize how wrong it was for me to be doing so many drugs because I was enjoying it. I finally began to realize I was completely out of control and overwhelmed by anxiety and paranoia because of people I called my friends and being reckless. I desperately needed to change my way of life.

Earlier that winter, my friend Frank told me skin popping cocaine was a good alternative to doing heroin. That same year, Sherry, a friend I had met years earlier at church, showed me a bag of heroin and asked if I wanted any. It was the straw that broke the camel's back. The brother of someone I knew had died from a heroin overdose, and I knew I could not trust the drug. I felt so stressed, and I did not know how to cope with all the bad mistakes I had made. But I would make the best of it and stay out of trouble by using what I learned on the streets.

I drove my family sick with worry. My mom and dad were completely frustrated and at their wits' end. Time after time they went to different mental and behavioral health agencies trying to find out why I never came home and when I did, why I was so high on drugs. They tried so hard to understand me. There was nothing I would have loved more than to have them help me. But nothing they did—the punishments, the groundings, changing schools—worked. I always managed to manipulate myself into even more trouble.

At the end of my sophomore year in high school, my parents asked Carl's parents, Anne and Domenic, if I could live with them in Maine. I didn't know that my parents were talking to them about me. I can remember sitting in Anne's kitchen when we discussed some of this, and she asked me to live with them in their home. Carl was excited at the possibility when we talked about it. Anne's daughter was a heroin addict, and Carl's parents caught him holding parties at the house during school hours.

It wasn't a good place for me to start a new life. Although this was a great opportunity to leave my family, I felt like I'd lost everything. I was under the impression my parents didn't want to deal with me or have me live with them. My father told me several times I had lost his trust and would have nothing but room and board. Arranging for me to live elsewhere made me realize I'd lost my family, and I was alone more than I could have imagined. I was in shock and devastated. I rose from the kitchen chair and walked out of the room saying nothing. I knew I was on my own. But then I ended up staying at home, and the subject was not brought up again.

My longing for friendship and to connect with someone was overwhelming. I didn't care about my future, grades, or activities in school. I did not want to go to college. My school curriculum did not challenge me enough, so I lagged behind. I needed help finding direction in my life. I had lost any dreams of being a better person or student. I was always alone looking for a place to go, but there was nowhere to turn. I had no healthy goals or role models. My parents were too busy ignoring me and punishing me with a curfew. I smoked pot—found in my father's dresser—with my friends, losing any bond I had left with my parents. My father held a grudge for many years and made good on his threat of only having room and board. No one noticed or recognized my day-to-day pain.

A combination of drug abuse, loneliness, and isolation equaled low functioning and no desire to succeed and live a happy life. I remembered my dreams when I was a young teenager, trying to hold on to something dear and special to me. But without help how could I? No good options were given to me so obviously I couldn't make healthy decisions.

My mother told me she thought there was something wrong with me because I was so compulsive in the way I worked in the kitchen. Basic day-to-day situations became a challenge. My mind was foggy from the drug abuse, and I became more stressed and confused. Anxiety began to control my moods. I suffered tremendous guilt for believing I was the cause of breaking up my family. I lost their trust and respect. I had a roof over my head. That was it.

I never felt responsible for all the destructive relationships in my life because I was young and naïve. But my self-destructive patterns were no one else's fault. I needed the strength to face my fears, take responsibility, and learn how to make healthy choices. I had a lot of making up to do. Some things I did, my disregard for my family, can never be forgiven, especially being in a political family. But my parents didn't completely give up on me. My mother found a drug counseling agency that took in troubled teens and told me: *If you don't do it for yourself, do it for us.* I said okay.

My drug rehabilitation sessions were torture. I was embarrassed to admit to my peers that I had a drug and alcohol problem. I never admitted to what extent I abused both. I was in denial. The need to run was foremost in my mind, because I could not deal with my problems. I was never sure what the depression and anxiety stemmed from. I just knew it was normal for me to experience this, and my mind began to play tricks on me. I was always fighting for reality. I thought I had to be strong, and my life would be better.

During my sessions I would hear voices that were not there. I would sit in therapy concentrating only on hearing my name announced over and over in a nearby park. I would hear without end my name over a sound system and then applause. This continued throughout the session. When I wasn't planning to run to Florida, I was so stoned at my counseling sessions they were just about a total disaster. Debbie, my counselor, got through to me, and I stopped getting high before my sessions.

I went to rehab for about six months and learned life goes beyond getting high and hanging out with bad people. I began to like who I was and to dislike anyone who offered me drugs. I learned anyone who offered me drugs was not my friend and didn't care about what was best for me. I wasn't facing the reality of the dangerous situation I was in. I could have been given bad drugs, forced to have sexual relationships I didn't want, been put in jail, or have a deadly overdose. I had problems in all my relationships, my faith suffered, my education and any goals I may have had were put aside.

When I said *no* I felt proud of myself and knew that relationship would end. I split up with most of the people I knew, including the drug dealers. Even though I stopped my sessions because I didn't believe they could help me change who I thought I had become, I did stop taking drugs but continued abusing alcohol for many more years.

During my recovery I felt I needed to make a new circle of friends, and I did. By not being excluded I began to appreciate life and living again. I felt relaxed and at times more balanced inside. I could enjoy their company more and enjoy life as I had not been able to for several years.

I was slowly able to replace what the drugs had taken away. I was into my art classes and doing home portraits. I enjoyed and participated in family leisure time like sailing and skiing. I began to develop healthy dreams. I read books written by Ernest Hemingway and wanted to hang out at Paris cafés with other artists.

It was less tense at home, and I started to look through college catalogs. Being a junior in high school, I wanted to go to the Rhode Island School of Design, study art, rent my own apartment, and earn an undergraduate degree in the arts or architecture. That was my dream, but the reality was I couldn't focus or concentrate on the applications and creating a portfolio seemed a monumental task

I was coming off drug and alcohol dependency. I had a number of confusing life changes that needed to be dealt with in therapy. I was frightened. I needed special attention and had no good way to reach out. I was completely overwhelmed, emotionally fatigued most of the time, and utterly confused. I tried to tell my friends, but they thought I was only stressed out.

It was a very lonely time for me because I felt unique in my experiences. If I could have only found someone to relate to and open up about this new life. To start over so quickly was difficult to do on my own.

Chapter 5

IT WASN'T FEAR of what the drugs were doing to my mind that made me change my lifestyle. My relationship with my family, friends, and my faith in God were destroyed. That was my motivation to quit. It was extremely important to me to mend the hard feelings I had created in my family as a result of the drinking, drug abuse, and the humiliation that went around it. The guilt was overwhelming. I could not make sense of so much. I felt so much loyalty toward my family, but my actions never showed it.

For a short while, my thoughts cleared, and I began to notice life more. It was a strange experience. I still felt like I was drugged; colors were more vibrant, and I was hypervigilant. My highs and lows were getting worse.

I broke up with Frank to have a new boyfriend, Brent. I met him hanging out at Morrison Park. It was not a healthy relationship. Brent was very jealous and angry and thought I was cheating on him. He threw a butcher knife at me from thirty feet away. He missed me but almost hit my girlfriend Cindy. He sped away on a motorbike with a friend. Later, he threatened that if I didn't sleep with him, he would tell everyone that I was a whore and I wouldn't be able to walk the streets of Medford with my head held high. I told him to go to hell. Losing no time he kept his threat, and the rumors started. Many people actually believed him. My friends told me anyone who knew me wouldn't believe it. But there were several thousand students in my school so how many could know me? The rumors grew worse. No one knew how to help if they wanted too. I felt as though I had lost all my friends and been put in social exile from my community. I was so traumatized I didn't date another man for four years. My relationships with men were never healthy. I never married because I never knew how to keep a healthy relationship; I always felt inferior to men.

One day I learned drug dealers were calling me a snitch, saying I was giving information to the police. That was a battle I couldn't win. I felt humiliated and hurt and learned who was a friend. Obviously, the kids who only showed hatred were on my shit list. I could not look anyone in the eye. If I did, sheer terror ran through me because I thought when I held eye contact, I would instantly kill that person.

I was suspicious of everyone in the school, and I would tell my friends that I had conversations with God. I stopped dating, and socializing. I kept a few close friends, none that attended the same school.

Several months before my senior year I went to Martha's Vineyard for a weekend on a cabin cruiser with two friends of mine, Gale and Lucy. Gale's mother and her boyfriend planned the weekend.

I became completely delusional, paranoid, hearing voices, and hallucinating to the point where it felt like I was looking through a kaleidoscope. I heard hundreds of voices within each hour of the day. It never stopped. The voices were so demeaning. They would call me a douchebag. I walked with Lucy and Gale and was terrified I would be shot dead.

I recall feeling tracked down by the Mafia and being

totally controlled by New England's godfather. One night on the boat we were all watching television. The picture on the television was showing a man facing backward on a director's chair. I was sitting on the same type of chair. I thought it meant the man on the television was controlling my life and knew where I was, what I was saying, and could see me wherever I was, doing whatever I did. It was sheer terror.

I thought I was special and cursed at the same time. I felt I had some sort of important purpose although I could never figure it out. I was blacking out constantly, without taking drugs or alcohol. One moment I would be at the bow of the boat and the next I would watch myself climb to the top where the wheel was. I lost time and felt terrified that I had no control from one moment to the next. It did not make sense to me. Time was lost, like amnesia or a fugue state.

I remember going to a restaurant with my girlfriends and becoming completely emerged in hallucinations. Before we were waited on, I thought I was biting into a hamburger with heroin in a purple pouch placed in the middle of the burger. I lost more time and only remember walking out of the restaurant.

At Martha's Vineyard we played quarters, which is a drinking game doing shots of whiskey. We were all pretty hammered. I had a good time for a while. When we turned in for the night, Gale and Lucy were laughing about things I did. I joined in on the laughter because my delusions told me to. I was uncontrollable. My friends laughed at me not knowing what I was going through.

I heard them say: "What is she laughing at?"

I had absolutely no emotional affect by the time the weekend was over. My dad had asked me how the weekend was, and I told him, with no interest or excitement, that it was okay. Later, he told me he knew there was something wrong with me by the way that I responded.

There are no words to describe the pain and suffering.

I would try to get everything just right. The dishes at home had to be placed in the exact order. If they were a fraction of an inch off, I would become completely frustrated and angry. My mom would watch me, and I thought she was thinking I was just awful. She didn't know what problems I was having.

I was completely overwhelmed, and my thoughts became disorganized. I thought I was responsible for the fate of the world. I thought I was possessed by the Devil, causing sheer terror to rip through me. I wore a huge silver cross for protection. One afternoon I visited my parish priest and asked for an exorcism. He said a prayer and sent me home. He did not contact my parents or try to intervene in any way.

I began to hallucinate visually; I would see rainbows that were not there and experience complete and utter confusion. My thoughts were distorted and grandiose. One day in class, in a complete frenzy, I contemplated committing suicide because I thought I had to die to save the world. I thought I was Jesus Christ. When people looked at me, depending on my day, it was either because I was special or because I was hated, and they were out to kill me.

Words appeared magically on paper, and I would trace them with a pencil before they could disappear. These words were meant to be the secrets of life itself. It was pure torture that my beliefs were so grandiose that what I had to do was unreachable. I would create meanings that held answers to my life. For example, my biological father was not related to me; the godfather of the Mafia was my father. He was God, literally, and I was supposed to do everything he said no matter what because he was also my father.

I cried out for help in subtle ways. One day I threw something at the kitchen window hoping to break it. I thought that would bring me some attention, and I could somehow tell my parents that I needed help. But the glass did not break. I was relieved because had the window broken, I wouldn't have been able to tell them how I was feeling. I would have been in serious trouble and would have had to make up an excuse about what happened. I didn't need any extra trouble.

I could not sleep, averaging two hours a night. I would hallucinate that the radio DJ was talking to me and giving me special messages.

Finally, less than two weeks before my seventeenth birthday, I lost it at the dinner table. I began to shout Jesus Christ over and over. I thought the Devil had entered my body, and I needed to fight with Christ to get him out. The first image that came to me was the scene in *The Exorcist* where Linda Blair's face turned demonic. I asked my sister if my face changed. She said yes. I thought she meant I looked like Linda Blair did. I was afraid to see my face all contorted.

My mom called the emergency line of an HMO, which was a relief. I thought she was asking them for help because I was possessed by the Devil.

This happened during my sister's first weekend home from her freshman year of college. She was so excited to tell us all about it, but instead, she experienced me decompensating. I was never able to say I was sorry and would try to make it up to her. It wasn't the first time I had disappointed her, and it wouldn't be the last. Her anger would simmer, and out of the blue she would lash out and hurt me.

The next day I missed school and went to see a psychiatrist. I don't remember what happened. Much of the next four or five months remain a blur. I was put on heavy medication and remember having extreme fatigue and awful side effects, including weight gain. My muscles would literally contort. It was embarrassing and physically painful. The doctors put me on more medication to stop the reactions. I was on high doses of haloperidol and thioridazine.

My mother thought our first therapist, Dr. Dulan, was good because he diagnosed me and answered all her questions. She told me this but didn't tell me what questions. He asked me what I thought was wrong with me. I told him I thought I had schizophrenia. I am clueless to this day how I knew. It was a guess. He told my family and me a little about the cycles of paranoid schizophrenia. He said I would have some very good days and some very bad. I would be lucky if they evened off. He said there would come a day when I would be in the supermarket and hear the voices, and I'd just think: *Oh, there they go again*, and it wouldn't bother me. He was right.

My first psychiatrist from our HMO, Dr. Rama, had given me no hope for the future and blatantly told me I would never feel good about myself, never have normal relationships, and never be able to work. Doctor Rama promised me a life of pure hell, one that I vowed never to live.

I thought: *Fuck you; I will have a normal life. I will be happy, have friends, go to work, and go to school.*

I told my mother many times I didn't like Dr. Rama, but my mother did for some reason, and I had to continue seeing her. This was the beginning of another fight separate from drug abuse and bad relationships.

After my first diagnosis my mother worked it out with the school administration to lessen my course load. I was home-schooled for about three months. I found it hard to leave my friends and my high school. I felt as though I had found myself in a comfortable place with my peers before I became sick, but then I received a diagnosis and was put on dangerous meds.

I decided to go to a tri-city school. I hated it. I thought it was a receptacle for losers and social misfits. I never considered myself a loser or a misfit. It felt like we were hidden away where no one knew because we were ashamed of ourselves. I felt as though I was not like the other kids.

Before my disability and drug rehab, I was well-liked and had so much fun partying with so many people every weekend. My nickname was Hurricane Bonnie, which referred to the Neil Young song. I was treated special everywhere I went. I felt so beautiful sometimes, inside and out. I looked back on the good old days and fought to be happy and alive again. I wanted so much to be liked, accepted, and have friends again. I wanted to date and socialize. My dreams were vital to my survival. I fought so hard to regain my dignity. I had to start over and rebuild my life.

During the first few months after my break, I could not stand to be alone for fear of the Devil. My mother took a leave of absence from work to be with me around the clock. She was wonderful. I asked them to keep me out of the hospital. Remarkably, they did. One night my parents began to help me learn how to manage being alone. They would write a note and leave the house for ten or fifteen minutes at a time. I do not remember how it worked out, but I appreciated their efforts anyway.

My mom listened endlessly. We talked throughout the day, sometimes with tears. She helped me continue schooling at home. She brought me to the doctor twice, sometimes three times a week. She never let on that she was just as devastated as I was. My mom was strong, compassionate, and caring.

At that point in time, my family and I were not referred to any family groups or advocacy agencies. We were basically left on our own. I received no constructive feedback on issues related to schizophrenia or how to deal with my emotional struggles. My concern about my family's reaction was so important to me. I received no help on how to deal with my losses. I can recall being very alone.

I was on heavy medications that did not help my symptoms. I had severe side effects and suffered from chronic fatigue and severe depression, which was never treated. All I could do was sleep. My neck contorted to the side. It was extremely painful. My mother called emergency services, and we picked up Benadryl. I was thought to be lazy. Little did anyone know I could not function at all.

The next few years were a blur, but I kept a journal that chronicles that time.

1/14/81

A lot of people think I have a lot of talent for sketching. I have been commissioned a couple of times to sketch other people's homes. I hope I do a good job. My dad seems to think I could make a living from it. I don't think so. If I did try, I wouldn't know where to begin. It is great, though, my dad having confidence in me, but I still picture darkness in my mind when I look into my future.

4/20/81

I opened my eyes and what did I see, but all these eyes looking at me.

It was hard to hide. The pain I mean. I was doing addictive drugs every day for so long. All I knew was that I felt better. Maybe it was the last home run, the last long stretch to sanity or reality. I wanted to desperately feel nothing, to hide the pain, to stop the guilt. Taking drugs did not in any way ease my pain. I put myself at serious risk of becoming a statistic. I stopped at age sixteen. I was lucky.

7/22/81

I used to remember every time I got close

*to someone, they would leave. I always had this
empty feeling. That is why I always turned to drugs
sometimes. They could fill me up.*

8/3/81

*I feel crazy today. It seems as though everything
is magnified by a hundred. Everything has meaning
beyond life. I try to find the meaning, but there is
nothing to grasp onto. I try to tell myself I have a
good head on my shoulders and not to search for
that higher meaning because there is none. It feels
like my mind is playing tricks on me. I am trying to
be extra tough and not let it totally consume me by
not thinking anything I normally would not and not
doing anything I normally would not. I know myself
well, and it gives me an advantage.*

*I took a sedative. It is helping. I'm paranoid. I
tell myself not to think or believe paranoid thoughts
so that they do not control me. This helps me relax
and think straight for a couple of seconds.*

*I feel like everything is too real. It feels like I have
been left with the stark realities of my life. This is very
difficult because I am making changes in my life. I'm
not desperate because I know I am strong. I know I
can turn my life around for the better.*

*My thoughts and actions are not my own
but controlled by other people. The intensity and
magnitude of the feeling are more than overwhelming.
I feel like my future will be determined by someone
else's actions because they bug my house and have
hidden cameras and snitchers in place.*

10/10/81

*I have to take a pill every two hours or seven
times a day. I have ESP. It is hard to control. That*

does not mean it is impossible, does it? ESP is the worst illness to have. I hear people's voices. It makes me so sick I create my own. I have the wildest hunch that other people can read my mind too. It is horrifying. It makes me depressed.

10/29/81

I feel a little better, more than anyone will know. I don't go to my high school anymore. I am hoping to go to a school in Malden. It is located under a church. I'm sick. I hear voices. It is bad and causes a lot of stress. The pain is bad. Donna from Arlington Catholic sent me a get-well card. She thinks I have mono. She wants to get together when I am well enough. Carl called. He wants to get together this Saturday. Don't ask me what we will do. I can't drink because I am on medication. I have not heard from my friends from my old school in a while.

11/13/81

I am finally beginning to accept the fact that I am sick. My family psychiatrist says I have schizophrenia. I am able to accept that my illness is a definite problem. I have been diagnosed with paranoid schizophrenia. I will still be able to go to school and have my studies and a normal report card. I am willing to do whatever it takes to get good grades. I definitely need the help, and I will get it from my new school.

So much has been going on. Hopefully it will disappear, the schizophrenia.

1/2/82

All I want to do is sleep. I am reading a good book, and the teachers get mad when I read because they think I am isolating myself. What do they know; I just really like the book.

I have not told Gale anything yet. I called her, and she was out. I called her a second time, and nobody was there.

1/4/82

Hi, I was talking to Gale. I told her I had a nervous breakdown and was going to a special school. Boy, you do not know how it feels to tell someone you had a nervous breakdown and have them say nothing, not a thing! I can't relate to her for some reason. I hate it, but I had to tell someone, especially her, because she would keep asking about school.

Did you go? Did you go? *she would say.*

I told Carl I have schizophrenia. He understood. His family does not want us to be together. His mom thinks it would be wrong for us to marry.

I want to make something of my life. I have to do my homework.

I don't feel like I fit in anymore. No one calls, no one pays any attention to me. I am a nobody, a freak to be laughed at. I can't get away from it! Someday I will. How can I?

My self-image has changed so much. I feel strange, not natural. I'm so paranoid. I feel like a demon to be destroyed. I have no more self-esteem. My life has been ruined. My reputation has been smeared all over. The rumors are awful. I can't trust anyone. I am paranoid. Try telling that to your shrink.

AFTER I LEFT MEDFORD HIGH SCHOOL, I finally started to tell others I had a nervous breakdown. I was treated like I had leprosy. The stigma was overwhelming. I felt as though I was totally shunned by my community.

A friend of mine had been diagnosed with bipolar when she was a sophomore in high school. She lived in West Yarmouth. We were so close and had known each other since grade school. When she disclosed, I said nothing because I did not know what it meant. Afterward our friendship suffered, and she became distant, competitive, and a drug addict. I never liked her again nor did I miss our friendship.

Now my friends reacted the same way to me when I told them I had schizophrenia. It was torture for me, and I felt responsible to my family. I thought my reputation reflected on them, so I had to set it straight. It became a lifetime challenge for me. My friends stayed away because they did not know what to do. I wish I had known that then. The isolation was too much for me to bear. I thought their silence was just from hatred, not helplessness and fear.

My paranoia was torture being around everyone at the high school because I believed everyone in Medford hated me and was bullying me. Everywhere I went I would hear obscenities over and over. Everyone I passed would say the same words; I heard it hundreds of times in an hour. There was no relief. It made me feel bad about myself, and I felt betrayed by all the surrounding communities. My doctors and family said what I heard wasn't real, but nothing could change my mind.

I can remember not wanting to take the medications. I was suspicious of my doctors and my parents and thought it was their way of having control over me. I felt abused and tricked. If I took the medication, they would win, and I would be just another fool, a loser to be laughed at. I wanted to be strong and save the world.

I was finally able to gain back my faith in God because my mind cleared enough to filter out some reality. I fought with every breath I had. Night and day I prayed to God to help me concentrate, to stop thinking and feeling paranoid. I felt it so deeply that I was in physical pain. It was always something I could depend on. My faith became a gift to me, and I always looked for my purpose, my strength. This gave me a new reason to live life to its fullest. I began another journey at the age of seventeen.

I stuck it out at the school in the basement of a church and received my diploma. Although it was not very fancy, the kids there turned out to be my friends. They accepted my disability and me. At times we had fun. We would listen to albums, do funky arts and crafts things, play pool, and cook our own lunch from scratch. I was the first to receive a diploma with highest honors. My favorite course was creative writing. I thought my teachers were cool. Many times I wondered why they would sacrifice so much of their time to teach us.

My family and I moved to the next town over about two years later. It was not far enough for me. I was put in shame, and my family felt ashamed also. There were times I still wanted to run. Just get in the car and go. The feelings were intense. I hoped and dreamed of moving to another state. This time not to run away but just move away, gain my freedom, my peace of mind. There were times I did not think this would be possible. I knew I would not be running from my problems. I would bring them with me.

A few years after I was diagnosed, my symptoms began to improve although I still believed I had ESP. I began to learn and understand myself and illness better. I always believed the voices were real, and that others could hear them. It was a tough obstacle to hurdle, but in time I learned to distinguish between what were really my voices and what were not.

As time passed, my value system began to change and grow. I felt a deep bond with my immediate family and with God. Even though I could not go back to my church, my faith sustained my life with courage and hope. Depending on God was something I knew I could always count on. He was my best friend and would never leave me. Later, my faith brought on my higher self, knowing that I could continue to strive to be a better daughter, sister, aunt, and a good friend.

2/20/83

My mother is uptight a lot. I blame myself for her actions and feelings. I could never completely understand her anger at me. It will never come to a resolution.

3/8/83

Sometimes I am afraid to think because someone is going to get really mad. I feel as though someone is going to kill me or make a fool of me.

4/83

I am experiencing conflict with my mother. She says some of it is imagined. It makes me feel like I can't separate reality from my illness. It kills me inside. I feel so much guilt. I hate myself for getting so mad and frustrated at her. I feel so much loyalty. It is hard to make sense of it all.

There are times others abuse the identity of my illness when we do not get along. If I become angry, I usually didn't say anything, but I would have a sour look and walk away. When I would do this, everyone would be so alarmed as if they are afraid of me.

After I graduated from high school, my mother got me a job at Home Owners Savings Bank in Boston. The heavy doses of medication made me so tired, and I could not keep a train of thought or remember how to perform my tasks. One day I was so exhausted I fell asleep in my chair. When I woke up, all the other employees were lined up, staring at me. I thought maybe I was snoring or something. I was eighteen years old, fired from my first job, and on unemployment. I looked in the *Boston Globe* every day for work but couldn't find anything.

My father told me he could get me a position as a secretary at the Massachusetts House of Representatives. I couldn't type well, but my father pressured me into it in less than thirty seconds. I started working full time. While there I gained good secretarial skills, made new friends, and paid room and board.

8/7/83

I am working at the State House and am making new friends. I still party with Carl every weekend. I have bad dreams every night. I am afraid to sleep. Sometimes at work they fill my head, and I can't concentrate on what I am doing.

12/28/83

You know, I try to hide the pain, but it always shows again. It is heartbreaking to hear it from my family. I feel like I am living in hell. I get hurt very easily. We hurt each other. I guess I am super-sensitive to others around me, but they do not understand me and show a lack of sensitivity toward me. I need to love someone and have the same returned. I need compassion in my life. It is filled with too much loss and grief.

I was about nineteen when I went to my first To Encounter Christ (TEC) weekend, which my parents set up for me. I felt a need to belong somewhere and to feel a connection with others. My mother thought this might help. After dropping me off at the Cenacle religious center, my mom and dad spent an exhausting two days praying for me, hoping not to receive a call to take me home. The TEC program was for single adults and had different weekends for men and women.

The weekend changed my life. I began to pray again without feeling delusional and paranoid. It felt natural and real. I stayed connected with the group and later formed relationships; some were the best in my life. It was the best thing my parents ever did for me.

A few years later I became a counselor for Catholic teens prior to their Confirmation. I was chosen to give a talk on Christianity in action as a counselor at a TEC weekend. It was wonderful. I talked about my experiences with life and my challenges and how I dealt and lived with a mental illness. After the talk everyone gave me a standing ovation. I felt accepted again, even though I had schizophrenia. My experience with the women at TEC was profound because society, I felt, was taught to hate and shun people like me.

It was there I met Maria, Mike, John, and about a dozen others. We would meet at Maria's house and have a few Heinekens. After an hour or so passed, we would pile into two cars and drive to clubs in Boston or somewhere close. I loved to dance. One night I danced with Sam. It was perfect; we could anticipate each other's moves before we made them.

1/16/85

I still have not developed good coping skills. I try to solve my problems, mostly emotional, but I always just dig up dirt that holds no answers. Talking does not help. I need a two-way relationship with my therapist. Why would I want to just sit and ramble on without any response or help? I don't.

3/16/86

I don't have time to be crazy. There are so many other things that are important to think about. I want to live a normal life.

I stayed at the State House for about three years before quitting because my secretarial job became boring, and I felt like I was at a dead end. I wanted employment that would make me more independent. Possibly to own my own business, like an art gallery or a clothes boutique.

Impulsively I went on an interview with the dean at Suffolk University. After looking at my transcripts, he suggested I go to a community college for a year then come back to see him. He told me he would remember me by the scarf

I wore around my waist. I enrolled full-time at Bunker Hill Community College.

When my dad found out what I had done, he was angry and said I'd blown it. "What will you do for work now?"

I told him I'd get another job, and I did. I paid him room and board every month.

I did well in my first semester at the community college. But then during the second semester of my freshman year, I stopped taking my medication and quickly slipped into psychosis. I was in complete confusion, doing and saying really weird things. Songs were played on the common room speakers that held the meaning to my life. I felt like people were talking about me and thought they could read my mind. I remember not being able to read my schedule, so I went into a random classroom, walked up to the teacher and whispered in her ear, asking if she knew where my class was. I did not wait for a response and walked out of the room.

I received treatment from my doctors and began the medication regime again. Having a full-time school schedule and part-time work was too much stress for me. As I continued on my medication, my thoughts cleared enough to function but with a lighter schedule. Amazingly, I earned good grades and was on the Dean's Honors List. I studied all the time. I would fight so hard to focus and worked until one in the morning. My exhaustion was overwhelming. No one understood why I canceled plans or couldn't keep up with household chores. I disappointed people, and my mother thought I was lazy.

I was trying to deal with so many confusing life changes, including college. At the time I worked as a nanny for our next-door neighbors. I needed to get to know myself and what direction I wanted to go in. My school counselors were no help. If my dreams were unreachable, I felt at a loss at what else to do with my life.

I received a high recommendation to go to Boston University—my first choice—from my school counselor at

BHCC. After going on an interview with a dean at BU, I was told that I would fit in perfectly. She told me that I needed to stay in a dorm for at least one year. My father complained about the cost of tuition, and I didn't want to deal with it, so I went to Suffolk University, a less expensive school, and commuted from home. My decision to attend a four-year college allowed me to believe I could accomplish something I was proud of and that I thought I might never have been able to do. My ideals were out of my reach, but even so, for a while my life took a positive direction, and I fought to enrich my life as much as possible.

I felt more assured that I deserved to be treated well by others and became more aware of the roles that I played. I met Mike through my girlfriend Maria from TEC. Mike and I dated for a short while and had some fun times together. We would walk along the Charles River, drinking a bottle of Schnapps out of a brown bag, carefree of any troubles. He introduced me to sushi, and we went to jazz bars. He spoiled me by buying me a beautiful, expensive dress from a boutique in Harvard Square. We became family, always there for each other in good times and bad. I have succeeded and failed at many relationships, but Mike is a constant in my life. I know that I have done my best to fulfill my needs in our relationship.

Relationships are complicated for me in any circumstance. Suffering from fatigue and depression made keeping plans difficult, so I canceled a lot. Compounded with my disability, it was a great accomplishment to discover and nurture a healthy bond with another. I needed to be less naïve about who I chose to share my life with. I was mostly hurt psychologically and emotionally. If someone wanted to change me because they found fault in me, it wouldn't be healthy. I felt I was never good enough.

While attending Suffolk University I started a series of part-time jobs. I was a certified home health aide, receptionist at Lesley College, waitress for a couple of weeks, and assistant teacher at a daycare center in Bedford, which I absolutely loved. I also did an internship from Suffolk. Along with school and work, I joined the Lexington Arts and Crafts Association and was elected vice-chairperson for the painter's guild. I continued art classes, sold artwork, and displayed work at local art shows.

Even so, I was in a constant state of turmoil and anxiety. I felt inadequate but had the desire to succeed and kept myself going. The transitions of normal life events—added to tensions at home that were never dealt with—made me feel overwhelmed, and my moods were completely unstable. I received no help from family or counselors. I didn't confide in Mike because I kept a lot to myself and felt alone and isolated.

I had always wanted to become completely independent, not relying on state or federal benefits. I believed it would keep my spirit healthy and would help me not define myself by my illness. I didn't know it would help make my illness seem less threatening. It would give me opportunities to take care of myself when I needed to. While living at home, my mother insisted I send for Section 8 applications to move out. I believed if I depended on federal housing assistance, I would not have the chance to start a career or live a normal life. If I did I thought going to college would be pointless because I wouldn't be able to use my degree. I needed help to learn how to live independently and feeling that it was going to be okay. I needed a dream to come true.

So I didn't fill out the forms and continued living at home while going to college, taking two or three courses at a time, and working part-time as much as I could. I perceived my mother had no hope for me. It seemed she had given up because she wanted me on public assistance. I was completely discouraged, not knowing what she wanted for me would be for the best. I was afraid of how permanent being on Section 8 would be and didn't believe I could make a decent life on my own. My stress levels would be so great I would have to stop everything for months at a time, still not knowing this is when assistance would help. I questioned many times the legitimacy of attending college. But I didn't want to be the type of person with only a high school diploma going nowhere. I believed college would give me that opportunity I so desperately needed.

I got the message she wanted me out of the house because she and my dad didn't want me to live with them. They didn't believe I was capable of doing it on my own. They were right, though I didn't want to believe I couldn't afford or handle the pressure of being on my own.

During my second year at school, I took an internship at Nynex, a technology company sponsored by Suffolk University. I went on an interview with their manager, believing I would be involved in marketing. But he asked me if I knew how to type. I was devastated knowing that I would be doing administrative work. It was a sales office with a high-stress atmosphere. The manager told the two other interns and me that this was a critical time in their jobs, and we should expect them to take it out on us. It took a lot of energy from me and began to break me down. My supervisor sent me to a copy store. While waiting for the documents, I was so upset I waited outside and cried. My stress level was so high I could not see straight. I went home and confided in my parents. My father suggested I tell my supervisor I had a blood disease and to quit the internship. I did.

I enjoyed my new group of friends, but I separated myself from them, too. Through my friends at TEC, I met John and dated several men at one time. John was the first person who made me realize I was a beautiful woman who deserved to be treated special and with respect by everyone. John showed me self-love without conceit. He was a close friend, and I valued his presence in my life because he never hurt me or put me down. He seemed to accept me as I was.

Even so, I decided to date another man, Mathew. I drove every night to his new apartment in Billerica. On a rare occasion he would pull up in my driveway and beep his horn. He never came to the door. After dating a few nice men and having such a good time, I settled with him, someone who did not like to do the same things I did. I spent nearly every night cooking him dinner, drinking beer, and watching television. I would have much rather been out dancing and being treated to dinner. He confided to me that he was an extremely violent man who had hurt innocent people in his past, possibly maiming them for life.

I couldn't accept how bad he was. He didn't get a reaction out of me. He told me one night that when he went home to his apartment, there were two people having sex in his bedroom. He retrieved his revolver from his bedroom drawer, went back to the living room couch and waited to put a bullet in my head. He thought it was me in the bedroom with another man, but it was another woman, a friend of his roommate. I didn't ask him where he was before he came home to his apartment or why he wanted to end my life if it had been me in his bedroom. It just seemed so strange because we never fought; we hardly talked, and I didn't know where his rage came from. I stayed with him for a short while after that incident. Coming back from a party, he told me he didn't care about me. I was so upset I cried until I reached my house. That was the end of our relationship.

Carl came into my life again soon after. He would patronize me, saying that there was something wrong with me because I did not love him and want to be with him for the rest of my life. He tried to convince me that no one else would love me as he did.

My life was explosive. I felt mistreated by others, and my college dreams were in shambles. I had to decide what course I wanted to major in at school. I had no idea what direction to take and received no constructive advice on how to begin to reach my goals from student counselors. I needed to explore what was possible and what I liked and did not know of any student groups that helped navigate career options. No one showed any caring or compassion, and my family life was intolerable. I was still living at home. I blamed it all on myself, but I didn't know what to do. I couldn't accept my limitations. If I did, I would believe I was a failure.

At that time I became a counselor at TEC. I disclosed my disability with a talk about Christianity in action. I felt my faith in Jesus was a good example to share with the women as far as I had been able to cope, despite having schizophrenia. I received a standing ovation and felt accepted, which I held dear to my heart. A month later I had all of my wisdom teeth removed, and my face swelled beyond recognition. Then my cousin Danny died of a drug overdose.

That was it. I couldn't take any more of life's shit or curveballs. At school I walked out of the classroom and in a complete frenzy had an angry meltdown in the women's bathroom. I went home and, in a panic, took an overdose of my medication. I did not want to die. I did not plan it. I was just out of control and did not know what I was doing.

About an hour later my mom came home from work, and I told her what I had done. She remained calm and immediately called emergency services. They instructed her to bring me to the hospital and to waste no time. My dad walked in, and my mom told him what I had done. He made us wait at the kitchen table while he looked through his medical books to read up on the drug I overdosed on. About a half-hour later, we went to the hospital. I had my stomach pumped and was admitted to the hospital for a few days.

I tried to convince my mother the suicide attempt wasn't because I was ill, but she wouldn't believe me. She told me I had always had such a love for life and could never do such a thing. I never forgave myself for not being able to convince her my life was going nowhere. I compartmentalized my stress and anxiety well enough to appreciate life, faith, and hope. Despite my faith, my spirit was broken. After a consultation with my parents, therapist, and psychiatrist, I chose to go to McLean's Hospital for two weeks. It didn't help at all. I made the wrong decision but thought I needed to go since I hurt myself.

10

3/5/89

    I just arrived at a psychiatric hospital. It frightens me. When I first arrived, I felt I needed someone to talk to. I was up and down and feeling anxious and very angry. I did not know whom to turn to. So, I went into my room and cried about what has been happening to me in the past eight months or so.

    I feel as though my suicide attempt has changed me, broke my spirit. Life doesn't seem like a gift from God to me. It does not seem like life will reveal those intimate surprises we receive at times and hope for more in the future. I used to love to live life to its fullest. I loved feeling everything around me and how I could set my emotions free. My emotions now are sometimes distorted and uncontrollable. I feel despair, disappointment, anger, confusion, and fear. I feel as though my spirit, my free spirit, has been broken. Will I ever love life through the eyes of a child? I will never be the same again. This one hurts too much. To be able to give up what Jesus gave me and not to want what he has to give to me in the

*future. I am broken and hurt. I don't know how to
be me again. I lost a good deal of my sense of self.
Will I ever see the woman I was again in the mirror?*

*I am scared for me. To live on an island,
isolated from freedom—my freedom.*

*I don't know how many times I can bounce
back without a part of me dying with it. I am going
to call John today and let him know where I am.
Maybe he'll visit.*

*I took an Ativan because it calms me down and
things bother me less. John told me he does not do
suicide. He left.*

I felt as though no one supported me. My therapist was not
there for me. She ended up leaving for her own practice. No
one helped! All they did in the hospital was re-diagnose me.
No one paid much attention to me or asked about my moods.
They just put me on new medications and called me schizoaffective. My doctor said one of the new medications would
prevent mini seizures I was thought to have because of my
blackouts. To this day, not one doctor could tell me what was
happening to me. But for some reason, I needed to be on the
medication.

I later understood my suicide attempt better, and now
know that it was my chronic stress and anxiety, but I had no
constructive ways to build a satisfying, fulfilling life I could
handle. I felt alone, hurt, and an overwhelming sense of hopelessness. I knew I was in trouble and could not do it alone,
again. The attempt unraveled feelings that I had suppressed
for years. I was so frightened by the attempt to take my life
that I felt compelled to analyze everything from childhood
to adulthood. My illness was part of me and something I had
to deal with. I was done fooling myself that I would not have

another episode. What terrified me the most was that it put me in so much anguish that at times my life seemed worthless and secondary. I took a temporary leave of absence from school and did not work.

3/24/89

It has been months since I have had over two hours of time to myself. It is so frustrating.

3/27/89

A someone so small
so sure
a great deal of life
a lack of will to live it
someone in the light
but no one calls her
words that mean nothing
to me
can drive me insane
rage of anger
means nothing
to one of any substance
wisdom means nothing
to one without the
ability to see
caring means nothing
to someone who lacks
the quality of
woman
or manhood
words cut so senselessly
are not for me to judge
but for you to
judge yourself
I wish you could

> *see yourselves through one*
> *who has God's eyes*
> *you would pity and feel*
> *snakes at your miserable*
> *head.*

4/1/89

It is hard for me to keep one thought. It is hard for me to concentrate. I don't know why I am alone now. So many things are thrown at me, and being so confused anyway, I can't make sense of it on my own. I think I am hearing voices. I hear things on the radio and television. But even normal people say it happens to them too once in a while. This is one of the worst times of my life.

4/14/89

Yesterday was an eight. Today is about a six. I have been thinking about God and how far I have put Him out of my life. It bothers me so much. I feel like my best friend has gone away for a while. When I was psychotic or paranoid, I used to be unable to change my thoughts. You know the difference between reality testing and crazy thinking. I would not let the distorted thoughts change my perception of what was really happening.

I want to do this when I am depressed without blocking out any of the feelings because I want to be able to deal with whatever is bothering me.

Material success means so much less to me than personal success. Being in love, having someone special in my life will take place sometime in my life. But right now, I feel as though I am in between progress and failure. I have to be a part of this world. People and friends mean a lot to me. But there has to be something more. I need to feel happiness inside me. I don't know if it exists.

Why am I so different?

6/21/89

My parents and I are not getting along. I went to Hyannis to get away for a while. When I came home from the Cape house, nothing was different for me. I still felt frustrated and full of tension. It's tough to be so torn.

I am afraid to start my career. I am afraid to move on my own. I am afraid to fail over and over. I have low self-esteem. I need to be on my own, but it is so hard to live at home as an adult. I need more encouragement. It hurts like hell. I can't leave on hard feelings. It is impossible for me. It makes me lose hope.

6/22/89

My mother and I had a long talk last night. I told her how difficult it is to live at home and that I am fed up with everybody. She senses the negativity and tension at home too. We talked about the expectations that people have of each other. I told her that I had dealt with that issue years ago. It's like you are in your own little bubble expecting things from others and not getting your needs met. I told her: How can you expect something from someone if they don't know what you want or not tell them how you feel about it? Your expectations of others will sooner or later fall short of what you want.

There's a way to get your needs met. It's just how you go about it. Telling someone how you feel or what you would like or need is a good beginning. You have to be assertive and remind yourself that most of the *time, others around you are not always tuned in to you. It is good to know your needs and how to meet them. But other people need to know what they are so that they can respect them.*

We also talked about accepting people as they are. I am beginning to do this. I don't put as much blame on myself that other people should be responsible for. I am trying to give myself more credit and not have people's negative opinions of me hurt so much. Knowing that you can't change someone is very important and that everybody is different. Changing yourself for you is healthy. Changing yourself for someone else usually is not.

6/26/89

Acceptance to me means learning new healthy coping skills. I hope for faith, courage, and a greater understanding of myself. I have needed so much support from my friends and employers, but my faith is what helps me keep hope.

I have learned that I will always suffer. I have also learned that I will always recover, each experience taking something from me and giving something new. To lead a normal, happy life with my disability, I need to keep experiencing healthy emotions. If I feel a void, I call a friend, put on relaxing music, pray for something personal, and change my attitude. My mood swings are usually what creates the vacuum, the void. I do not know how to deal with certain parts of my life, like loneliness and depression.

John made my life complete. I felt an inner balance and beauty, love for myself without conceit. Other people would spark curiosity in me. Life was a joy. I was happy. With disappointment, comes hope. Hope is eternal, not disappointment.

7/2/89

My sister and I have grown so far apart. I miss the buddy, hang around stuff. At least for now we are not as close as I wish we could be. I am so affected by the loss of our companionship. I admire her so much and miss her friendship.

7/19/89

My situation with my family is intolerable. I am suffering so much. It has been more difficult as time goes by, and no one admits there is a little tension. I am going to stick it out as long as I can. I need to earn my degree. Today is a rough day. On a scale of one to ten, it is about a three or a four. It is because I am not getting along with my parents, and my symptoms are getting worse. They make me feel uncomfortable about who I am, so I hide my emotions. They have formed a distorted impression of me. It is demeaning and hard to deal with. It is mostly non-verbal and emotional.

8/26/89

I need to develop good coping skills to survive. I have been trying, but I still feel at a loss. Sometimes I can cope well, and sometimes I come up short. It amazes me how much my family's conception of me can play such a big role in how I feel about myself. The stigma attached to having a disability is overwhelming and devastating. My parents and Layla took away everything I am. Either they don't expect anything from me, or they are at a huge loss at what to expect. It is living hell. The best way for them to learn is by talking with me. I'm broken, so I have no answers.

I know what I want and that is to learn how

to deal with my stress and anger at home. I have started by doing small things like keeping my head together or trying to keep a small sense of peace of mind. Oh, it's so hard. I also want to keep my family in family meetings. I stayed because I thought if I got better, my family would be happier and enjoy life. I needed a college education to survive. My father was paying the tuition every semester. This was the best way I could earn my degree, so I sacrificed my independence.

10/89

I felt helpless for too many years. I needed love and understanding, but I couldn't get it from my family. I was just a loser and a troublemaker. My father told me that things were never going to be the same. He blamed me for ruining any further political life he could have had because of my bad reputation and mental health problems. I should not have hoped for more because things were never the same again. I had to deal with my problems on my own because I knew that trying to have my parents understand me would be impossible. To them my problems are my problems. Not that all I ever wanted from the beginning was to be able to talk with them and hope to settle some within myself.

When I do move out, maybe my parents will feel relief and respect me more as a capable person.

My family values were constantly being threatened. I felt I should honor them and stay loyal, no matter what they did or how much they hurt me, but if I lost my sense of values, what would be left? To me nothing was left except pain and suffering. I needed a respite from all the confusion and madness. I knew this. But to put my family life back together meant going against what I had lived for, my meaning and purpose in life.

Some people, most people will not understand this, but blood is thicker than water. I thought if I got better, they would be happy. It's a hard lesson to learn that my family was less loyal to me than I was to them. They can help themselves without me. I wish I could take better care of myself without feeling the pain and the guilt. I want my life to change. I honestly did not believe I deserved to be abused by my family. They did so in many ways. I went without breakfast every morning. My mother never fed me. I sat under a bridge one day before school and ate my lunch because I was so hungry. Every day I had one sandwich and a dime for milk.

4/15/90

Dear John,

A year and a half ago, I felt the innocence you were talking about. The innocence and the childlikeness you saw in me that I never saw in myself. I felt estranged by the world because I could not understand why people react to me the way they do. It was either good or bad. My therapist told me it had to do with my moods. I have never looked at a person and judged them so harshly. Knowing spite on one hand and my strong religious beliefs on the other left me sad when I realized how other people can be when they are so empty and full of pain. I saw the other side, and I felt their pain. I can understand the void, the emptiness they feel. I do not have the words to put it in. I needed people too much, so I could not depend on myself to be happy. I never knew I could take control of my life. I am working on this now, and I feel I believe so much more in myself, and I feel competent, and I feel as though even though I have lived through an illness, I believe in myself and live a normal life.

Most of the time I didn't know how I managed all the stress and anxiety. Compartmentalizing and using complete focus and concentration helped me deal day-to-day but I was falling apart. I didn't know who to trust. I went to therapy. It didn't help because I was afraid to be honest. That was a mistake. I was terrified they would put me in a hospital where bad things happen to the patients.

I felt humiliated and disregarded because my family blamed just about everything on me and my illness. There was a level of anger and resentment toward me and that weighed heavily on my shoulders. My reaction to the trauma kept me home and allowed my family to blame everything I thought, felt, and experienced on my illness. They would humiliate and disregard me because I wasn't real. Their level of hate and bitterness was taken out on me.

A friend I dated when I was about nineteen later told me he didn't think I would make it out of my mother's house. He was invited to our Cape house in West Yarmouth. He was a good guest. My parents let us sleep in my bedroom alone. It was so weird, and I had the worst nightmares all night. I had wished he slept in a separate room.

My faith in Jesus and that He is Lord, and that He blessed me with the innate ability to love, to love life, to embrace its rewards and challenges, and the struggle to find love in relationships was then—and is now—the key to my healthy spirit. The most rewarding gift that God has given me is having the knowledge that people are not all bad, and that life can be wonderful and full of little surprises that mean more than any financial success could ever bring. I laid my head down every night and prayed for peace of mind and for real love to enter into my life. It kept me going and alive for many, many years because I truly believed I would be thankful in the end.

Finally, after using every way I could think of changing myself, none being successful, I was told nothing would change around there. Looking back, it was good advice because I finally learned at a deeper level that change needed to come from inside myself and that I would never be able to change anyone else. I needed to find what changes I could make then I could move on.

The hurt was great. It completely stopped me from any progress whatsoever. Once I began to move on and settle with what it would be like not to have the love, respect, and trust from the ones I care most about, scared me to death. How would I be able to live on without them, the people I had dedicated my life to love and care for, the ones I forgave every day and prayed for every night.

Suffering so much and sacrificing so much every day just brought me spiraling down further and further. My values kept me close to sanity as much as possible. I thought it was worth every ounce of pain to fix my broken family. The guilt I felt was beyond words. I blamed myself every day. I lived two lives, maybe more. Being different with my family than I was within other relationships hurt because I knew they only saw one side of me. A side I didn't even like. So they judged me. I felt torn and longed to be their friend. My relationship with them was never complete. It was limited. They rarely saw me interact with anyone but their friends. I was always quiet and never joined in the conversation. My mom thought I was only good at socializing with one maybe two people at a time. How wrong could she be? But I lived with it, never correcting her. I didn't know the pressure my father was putting on my mother to have me move out. He loathed me being there, hurting their marriage.

4/22/90

My family life has cut deep and has scarred me. I know that we all love each other very much but trying to live with each other is impossible. There is a lot of tension and feelings of frustration. None of this is talked about. It is swept under the rug. Even though I have always been down-to-earth and straightforward, I find it difficult to even find the words to tell them what I think.

4/22/90

I don't want to start worrying because I weigh only ninety-five pounds, and if I worry anymore I think I'll die.

6/11/90

My parents just buried me deep last night. All of my feelings and losses toward my family cause me to hear voices, and I cannot focus on reality. I become extremely angry and deal with it on my own. It is so disappointing. When I feel all the grief and guilt, I feel hopelessness. My disappointment brings on helplessness. I am because of them. Something inside me dies every time I even have a bad thought about them. My spirit breaks, and I feel nothing but despair and envision total darkness with no chance of seeing sunlight.

Since the day I tried to commit suicide, I may still have distortions, but I am aware of when I view life and people this way and stay away from it. I survive this way. I have come to terms that I cannot please anyone unless I take care of myself and learn how to like, love, and respect myself again. I hope to love life and others and that my spirit may become healthy.

What means most to me are my personal successes. I want to choose my life, my career, relationships, and talents, and all that goes along with it. My father taught me to never go to bed with something important unresolved. A good thing came out of this for me; I paid attention to the limits I set in relationships and prayed hard to God I would be okay.

11

MY MOM ATTENDED MEETINGS at a mental health support group for families and significant others who live with mental illness. She would tell me all I am is my illness. She was dedicated to the group and asked me to attend a session. I did and found it educating. My mom's friend Jack instantly took an interest in me because of the questions I asked. Later he approached my mom and said he wanted to do a film on me because I was so articulate. He wanted the subject matter to be how I managed an illness and how my family responded to me, their friends, and the community.

She asked me and I said yes. After my mother prodded Jack a few times, he finally came to the house. When he sat beside me, I instantly opened up, telling him a little bit about my experiences. That was all he needed. Jack was a filmmaker and decided to film me and my family just talking about mental illness in the family, about recovery, and what it was like for Layla to have a sibling with a mental illness.

It took a few years to produce what is now *The Bonnie Tapes*. The tapes made an impression, and I made a difference in other people's lives by giving them hope and encouragement. I felt it was my moral obligation to society. The tapes were considered groundbreaking because they were a unique tool for families to facilitate a discussion about their loved one's suffering from mental illness. The tapes spread worldwide, giving encouragement to thousands of family members and professionals to help people who have mental illness issues. The tapes are a tool for others to discuss openly what it really means to the individual and their families to deal with the struggle. Families and their loved ones were more often than not at a loss on how to approach the issues most important to help everyone who was affected. *The Bonnie Tapes* are on the shelves of mental health clinics, agencies, libraries, hospitals, universities, and homes. The tapes are groundbreaking because at the time there was no educational tool available for families. It shared an honest, open, and unscripted dialog of our family dynamics that many other families and professionals could use as a guide knowing that recovery is possible. We had no idea what questions Jack would ask us. There was no second take. As Jack told me, it was risky, but it worked out.

The reaction of my family on the tapes didn't come as a surprise. My mother made a comment on judging people and made a helpless gesture. Layla took a lot of convincing to be taped. I didn't know how my illness had affected her. She was completely traumatized thinking she had to be the perfect one, to make up for me. There was no discussion as a family on the tapes whatsoever after they were publicized.

I experienced no hate or dislike because of the tapes. I spoke at many groups and was welcomed everywhere. That had a profound, lasting effect on me. I was so proud to help so many others just by sharing my experience.

A few years after being diagnosed I was working full time, looking to go to school, and making quality friendships. It bothered me that they didn't acknowledge how my recovery was coming along in such a positive way, though Layla mentioned I was strong and didn't know if she could handle what I went through.

Even so I had a struggle in me that cut deep. I had just gone public about a part of my life I was secretly ashamed of and which at times I thought had ruined my life. I lived with this inner conflict, pushing it aside when speaking publicly about it. I received the Silver Ribbon Award and two certificates of appreciation from National Alliance on Mental Illness chapters. I thought I had achieved my personal success.

I met a lot of people from all economic groups, some of whom I socialized with. I spent days with an amazing woman I met from a group at Boston University. I would catch the bus and train to visit her in Boston. I stayed for three days straight on one visit. Oh, she made the best fried chicken!

When the tapes finally came out, I was still in school at Northeastern University attending classes at night and working during the day. My major was psychology. I wanted to learn about people and what made them tick. I enjoyed learning. School was always a joy to me. I was able to study for ten years and did well. At a seminar that included excerpts of the tapes, I met a woman who offered me a job before I graduated from college.

After graduation I learned to deal with one issue at a time and to take small consecutive steps to put change into practice, much like learning how to study. My life became easier when I began to deal with one thing at a time, beginning with the most important first.

It was mainly due to having remissions that I was able to separate who I am as a person and what the symptoms of the illness does to my thinking, behavior, and feelings. When I had first become acutely psychotic, there was no *me* left. Or so I thought. I began to empower myself by completely rejecting society's stigmas. My belief system about who I was had been challenged. My attitude changed from what judgments society accepts and being a victim of a brain disorder to a whole person who could function well in all areas of my life when I was well. It took decades of compartmentalization—putting aside issues I could deal with later and letting myself deal with whatever I could at the time—and do well.

I graduated and began my career as a residential counselor. My first assignment was in Mission Hill, Boston. It was challenging. The homes were owned by the Department of Mental Health. The clients were severely low functioning. The staff and I would cook for about fourteen clients and help them on issues they may have toward some sort of recovery. Several months later I transferred within the company to Swampscott and commuted to the North Shore for the 3:30 p.m. and 11:30 p.m. shift. I felt as though my job was secure, the staff was friendly, and the pay was enough for me to live on my own if I worked overtime once in a while.

I found an apartment across from the beach in Swampscott. It was a great location. I lived on waterfront property and lived five minutes from work. On hot days I would hit the beach at 11:00 a.m. or so and at 3:00 would go back to my apartment and get ready for work. By 3:30 I was at the front door of the residence I worked at. I felt so proud in the beginning. Then soon an overwhelming sense of negativity consumed me. I hated it.

Jack, the producer of *The Bonnie Tapes,* and I developed a close relationship. He was like my second dad. He would listen to me endlessly, and help me keep a positive attitude, which would at least get me through the day. He was there for me unconditionally. He would take me to his Wellfleet home on Codman Point, where I met Loren and Josh. We would go sailing with his son Ted and his friends, and we would eat raw oysters caught on the beach. It was wonderful. Jack and I would light a fire in his fireplace, share a glass of wine, and talk or read. There was no television set. It was perfect. Jack promised me royalty checks each month from the sale of the tapes. Loren was also involved in producing the tapes. We became close friends. When we went for coffee there wasn't a minute we couldn't fill our conversation. I met her at Jack's when we spent a weekend together at Codman Point.

I was thirty-one and on my own for the first time. I was not able to let my past go and move on. I did not have the strength and experience. My life could not be put in perspective and neither could my emotions. I let people take advantage of me at times, and it was difficult to deal with.

I loved the first six months of the job in Swampscott. My favorite part of working was talking to the guys and giving them my best advice and lending an ear or two when they needed it. The other employees were jealous, so some said. Irene, a woman who used to work there, told me to hang on because the clients can tell who is genuine or not, and I was doing a wonderful job. She told me the other girls who worked there were on a different level, and I would never understand where they were coming from.

A few months after I rented my studio, I stopped taking some of my medication to help anxiety and stress. I began to hate my job and started looking hard for something else. I would get up and spend hours sending out résumés. I was looking for a job where I could advocate and counsel.

The dynamics of the residence changed. Two men moved out, and two new men moved in. There were times it felt out of control. I was alone on most of my shifts. That scared me because one of the men would have violent outbursts at least three or four times a week. One night the police came to the door because of an outburst he had in the neighborhood. Neither my boss nor anyone else seemed to think it was a problem having a woman working alone under that type of circumstance.

My boss told me I could get a better job than the work I was doing. Everything seemed okay to me at work, but when she said this I felt she was pushing me out for a reason I didn't know. She never came to me with any complaints on my job performance. I requested overtime, and she created time for me on the weekend to take the guys out somewhere they would enjoy themselves.

I had a few deaths in the family. My maternal grandmother, who I felt particularly close to, and my paternal uncle died within a couple of weeks of each other. I was grieving for the loss of my relatives. Then I came down with pneumonia. It hung on for months, and my boss was irritated that I took so much time off. I lost my job, and my dad told my mother to bring me home. I was not on any housing assistance while living in Swampscott. An inner voice would always tell me that I could make it without depending on the state and federal government no matter what. I would always strive for complete independence. It was a good experience for me to find out what it was like to struggle on my own. I learned it was too expensive, and I couldn't afford it on my salary. Taking care of my health took precedence.

When I moved back home from Swampscott, my mom talked to me about their marriage. It was surprising for her to be so open and honest. I moved back home when my parents were taking care of their marriage. My head started to spin at the thought of my life and how complicated it seemed. I was beside myself with complexities in my life similar to what I had in college. There was no relaxing in sight, plus the pneumonia held on.

The Bonnie Tapes soared with popular acclaim and brought me some celebrity status. Through Jack I was able to meet the commissioner of the Massachusetts Department of Mental Health. She had heard about me through Jack and *The Bonnie Tapes* and wanted me to kick off her anti-stigma campaign. I chose to be part of her task force for Changing Minds, the anti-stigma campaign she had sponsored. My name was printed on the front page of the *Boston Globe's* Metro Section, announcing that I would attend a press conference for DMH. It also disclosed my experience with mental illness.

As the first speaker I was introduced as a wonderful woman and given so many accolades by the commissioner. My presentation was taped by all the major television channels in the state. After all the presentations I worked the room, made connections, and my career took off.

After the kick-off I met with the commissioner. She asked me what my career goals were and wanted to offer me a job. My mind went blank; I was so nervous I could not tell her. She suggested a few, but I was not interested. She told me to think about it and let her know. In response to her request I wrote her quite a long letter on issues I'd like to see changed in the system. As a result, she put me in touch with a politically influential agency that was a strong advocate for people who live with disabilities.

I was placed at the head of the consumer movement and worked with the Massachusetts Association for Mental Health (MAMH) as a public policy associate. They had close affiliations with the commissioner, politicians, and other agencies and people holding great influence and power. We raised $3.5 million from the state legislature for a housing initiative for DMH called People Are Waiting. We met with the budget director of the Massachusetts House of Representatives, sent out brochures, and talked with the governor and his staff.

I made connections and went to meetings, sat on a board of directors for a new consumer agency getting off the ground, and traveled the state and the country talking about the housing initiative and *The Bonnie Tapes*. I was invited to many conferences to speak on panels and gave lectures at prestigious graduate school programs. I held a position on the president's committee on mental health and employment. It was held in D.C. and three other executives from the Department of Mental Health joined me. We were expected to implement plans and strategies we made to our home states. I did this and held meetings with agencies specializing in mental health and employment and made suggestions to better aid their clients.

I held several positions that enabled me to meet more people and allowed me to develop a healthy network and resource system. I received several awards of appreciation and the Silver Ribbon Award for my participation on *The Bonnie Tapes* and my advocacy for people who live with mental illness. When people came up and gave me a hug to say thank you for the hope and inspiration I had given them, it was priceless.

Before I worked at MAMH, a friend had offered me the opportunity to take part in a recovery workshop at Boston University, so I decided to put off full-time work to take the course. It was the first time recovery was put in my vocabulary. That was when I realized I deserved no blame for my illness. The relief was breathtaking.

I was unfortunate to have a brain disorder, which could have occurred at any time in my life. I always thought I had caused my disability. The guilt was indescribable. I would always look to the past. *What did I do wrong? Could I have changed my destiny?* The answer is no. What is so sad is that I had always felt responsible for my parents' happiness and misery. I even felt responsible for their failing marriage.

I knew now I was not responsible for them and was able to enjoy at least bits and pieces of my life again. My faith, friends, and a new appreciation for others emerged. I realized not everyone is bad. I'm not bad. My family is not bad. We were dealt a heavy hand, and we were not alone.

The workshop touched on all the emotional issues you can think of. It was always right on the mark. It was a painful experience at the onset, but I learned what was important to me, and what was not. It made me think hard about the basics in my life. It was not simple stuff. Most of it was complex but so incredibly necessary. Through taking the course for eight months, I learned coping skills I will never forget— or could have ever gained—had I not decided to make a commitment to it.

I found it life changing because I felt a sense of trust, understanding, and respect. I needed someone who knew a lot about life and who took mentally ill people seriously. I began to accept my illness and what it does to me and that it would never change. I had tried to hide it from myself for so many years. It had been so painful to say the least. I was at peace with it, finally.

It's a common misperception that people who live with a mental illness are always irrational and have not learned how to control their impulses and emotions, which is untrue. I've met so many who live with disabilities all along the economic spectrum. One woman who I met at the YMCA was brought to tears telling me her story. She had a bright career and a home. She became ill and lost everything. She was unable to regain all her losses. Her sadness was profound. I had friends who witnessed the lynching of their family and had several personalities because of it. Yet another friend came from a wealthy family she did not fit into. Her whole life she just wanted them to understand and respect her as a person and member of the family.

About a year passed, and the pneumonia I contracted while living in Swampscott persisted. The health care agency had misdiagnosed the spot on my lung. I went to Lahey Clinic and I was diagnosed with a lung tumor. The cardiologist said that I was too young to be there. He then told us that I had a tumor in my lung and talked about radiation and chemotherapy. I was diagnosed with spindle cell carcinoma. They never told me I had lung cancer. I don't know why. I found out through my medical records. My parents had a responsibility to tell me. They said it was benign. I had no chemo or radiation. Luckily the cancer never returned, but I contracted COPD when I was fifty-four years old.

I was operated on within two weeks at Lahey Hospital. I had a lengthy stay and don't remember most of it. When I got home my mother took care of me around the clock. I received dozens of cards, and all were hung in my room.

It took about five months to fully recover from the surgery. I was forced to apply for Section 8 housing and was certified in a short couple of months. I couldn't take a breath to sip my morning coffee without my mother pushing me to look for an apartment.

I talked to the director at MAMH, and he took me back on a part-time basis. My recovery from lung surgery was quick. I took a vacation in California to visit my aunt. I had a great time. We connected, bonded in a special way. She is the greatest. My thoughts are always with her. She has kept love in her heart for the ones she cares about. I love her with everything I have. She is an inspiration to me, a role model.

Shortly after, my mom was diagnosed with cancer—liposarcoma, a type of soft tissue sarcoma. Her surgery was nine hours. In December while she was still recovering, I had to move out. I was crushed. My mom would not let me stay at home to take care of her, so I left for my new apartment in Arlington.

My mother's sister stayed with us for about three weeks to take care of my mom. She was showered with cards and phone calls. She was too weak for anyone to visit. Layla and I started to share our feelings about Mom and how we felt about her. My dad went through a tough time.

During my last stay at home, there were often times I felt that my mom and I would change roles. Too much happened during that year, and I don't remember most of it. My dad never talked to me about why I moved home from Swampscott. He just took me in. I guess that is what dads are all about; at least that's what my dad did. I developed stringent standards from the emotional trauma. I neglected this part of my life.

My father put me on the Section 8. I had four months to

find an apartment, went back to my old job, and was able to stay in my new apartment in Arlington.

I was out! I felt young and full of energy and thrived on my own. I bought designer suits and black, lace up artillery boots. Personally, I struggled with fatigue and continued to try to find complete balance. On a good day I would sit in the morning, with the sun shining on me through the window knowing I had everything I looked for. My friend Jack told me I am like a cat; I always land on all fours.

I turned around big time and relied on myself. I appreciated all the friends I met at the workshop because it was so hard to find others in my life that understood and would listen. They are few and far between. I found safe places to open up and spill my pain. It felt wonderful, perfect, and safe. It changed the way I perceived the others who would not listen and who were not there for me during good times and bad. I kept in touch with some, and others I had already known.

After I moved my mom got depressed. There was no one to take care of her except Dad. He would leave her alone a lot, and she could not take it. Somehow, he finally got the message, and for the first time in thirty years I saw him try to do his best by her. They took an impromptu vacation to Florida to visit friends.

I realized: *Hey, I have to take care of myself. They are responsible for their relationship, not me.* If there was a crowning moment or realization, it was this.

My education was so important to me. I was told getting a college degree would change me into a better person, but I struggled to stay employed. It has taken me years to learn how to go to work when I am at my worst and hold my own. It became easier to be professional at work on these days. It was the choices I made and how much—or how little—I let myself be real at the moment. I have learned that I have control in my life; control that I never knew was there.

To be able to deal with my disabilities and dysfunctions along with a shitty day seems like an accomplishment in itself. My sense of resilience has been impaired. Because of this, people don't understand. They don't have the tolerance. The meds make me feel tired and numb. I call myself the town drunk. It's a scary feeling to experience and to accept, never mind admit. I am still not completely sure why I feel this way or how to change it. I am still learning good coping skills and talking always helps.

12

DURING MY DAYS WORKING AT MAMH, I was contacted and commissioned to speak at the annual Taunton State Hospital Conference. I spoke on stigma; I was thirty at the time. The following is a brief part of the presentation I gave.

Stigma is a hateful word. With the mention of the word, it strikes a chord in every one of us whether we have been a victim of it or not. Stigma is abusive. Abuse is against the law. The words **STIGMA** and **DISCRIMINATION** are not new to me. I felt as though my community had exiled me. I felt hated and ignored by my friends. I would hear people calling me obscenities. It never stopped. My doctors called them voices. The voices were degrading. I would hear them hundreds of times over an hour.

Finally, after one quarter of my senior year, I decided to go to school in the basement of a church in Malden. It was a tri-city school. I hated it, but I wanted to earn my high school diploma. I was put in with what I thought were the misfits. My self-esteem was poor. I was sure my reputation was totally destroyed. I misinterpreted peoples' reactions toward me. I could not separate my disability from who I was. I thought everyone knew I had a breakdown, even strangers that I passed on the street. I always felt shunned.

I am not angry or bitter. My outlook is far from schizophrenic. Life is so short and too precious to waste on unhealthy and negative attitudes. To miss those small surprises in life, and not to appreciate what I have been given would take away the essence of my life.

My reality has changed. I have learned a lot about myself because my life has been full of challenges. When we overcome our obstacles, there is a lot to be learned. There are days I find it difficult to manage my stress and my symptoms. To get through the day, I reality test by bouncing my thoughts off someone I trust and who I know will give me a straight answer.

Being sheltered and overprotected is the worst way a person can treat someone with a serious mental illness. We all struggle with our identity and our reality. Fighting for a reality we can live with that feels natural is key to recovery. It is so unfair and grossly abusive to teach someone to be helpless just because they have a disability. What are people afraid of? We are not violent, bad people. When we become empowered, our first plan is not to kill our mothers and fathers and to sue our therapist. All we want is a chance to prove ourselves and earn back some respect that we've lost. People who live with a disability surely did not ask for it. We suffer enough because of the illness. And yes, we do know better. If we don't, we learn what is acceptable or not.

People who do not have a disability are unique to each other. Everyone has different success drives, levels of intelligence, interests, and character flaws. Take these normal people and give them schizophrenia and see how they handle their life. You will get just as many different levels of coping as there are people in the world.

The moment someone in my life learns that I have a mental illness, they stereotype me. When I break the norm of what our society thinks crazy should be, I get a mixed reaction. They do not see the person who has strong morals and values that are lived by every day. They do not know how strong my belief in God is and how my loyalty to my family gives me such inner strength.

Every time we judge someone, which we all do at times, it is wrong. It is like writing someone off before you even get to know them. The joy and experiences that could be shared are lost. There are days I feel victimized by stigma, even when I have come so far. I know that some would love me to act crazy. Others would like me to pull off the impossible. I wish they would get a clue. I am not a stranger to cruel rumors, hate, and jealousy. Some people think I should fight the world. I can't fight the world, nor do I want to. I just want to make it a better place to live in.

I have learned what parts of my personality are due to a disability, and who I am. To have others treat me like a child, and to feel helpless is educating and sad. Stigma is feeling like you cannot speak out. Many people are afraid to live a better life because they do not know when their disability will strike. Society is not equipped to handle working, educated people who live with a mental illness. The stigma is so great that these people do not take any chances to live a better life. They are the silent ones. It shouldn't take so much courage to want to live beyond poverty and oppression.

Times have changed. People have learned over the years that it is wrong to discriminate against minorities, the blind, and the handicapped, to mention a few. We should be asking ourselves

why, in the twenty-first century, do we discriminate against people who live with a mental illness?
It is not due to character flaws or because of poor
upbringing in childhood. It is a disease of the brain,
which can be alleviated, brought into remission by
the treatment of psychotropic drugs and therapy.

I would love to be married and raise a family.
There are people out there who do not believe
people with psychiatric disabilities should have a
husband or wife and have children. Why not? We
can function in today's fast-paced society. We can
work, cook, dress in style, and have nurturing relationships. As people who do not have a disability,
we love to love, and love children. Just because
we were born with a disability does not mean we
cannot live normal lives. There are so many bar-
riers out there in front of us from day one of our
diagnosis. It is tough to reach realistic goals, but
many of us do. I may never be able to stop taking my meds for nine months. When I am married I would like to adopt. I have wanted to adopt
children since my early teens. It would be such an
uphill battle; I may be seen as unfit because I have
a schizoaffective illness.

My first experience with the mental health
system after I was diagnosed was extremely dis-
couraging. My psychiatrist told me I would never
have normal relationships, would not be able to
return to work, and would never feel good about
myself. She was wrong. I have several friends who
love me unconditionally. And I feel the same way
about them. There is nothing we would not do for
each other.

I have an extended family. Colleen, my second
mom, is one of the best friends I could ever have.
I grew up with Colleen and her family. We have a
mutual fan club and can talk about everything; the
same with my aunt Lo. She is so special to me. I can

tell her straight about everything. When I am having symptoms and confuse it with what are stress, reality, and my disability, she tells me. I treasure the people in my life.

I have learned about self-love without conceit. I like myself, usually. I have bad days, and sometimes my stress is hard to manage and I don't always like how I come across, but I don't hate myself.

I had a psychiatrist and therapists who did not try to help. They just sat there thinking I liked to hear myself talk. I laugh at the absurdity. It angers me to know that I had to cope and deal on my own. Neither my family nor I were referred to any outside agencies or given any helpful advice. I never had a case manager. I could not show any anger because therapists view it as a symptom, not a person who has been abused and neglected by their family, friends, and society. The fear of being hospitalized is real and breaks more spirits.

While working as a residential counselor, I knew someone who was put in the hospital then placed in a community residence for the mentally ill because he was pissed off at his therapist. I spent five, sometimes six, days a week talking to him. In my heart I truly believe he is a victim of the cruel side of mental health. He is a wonderful person who felt as though he could not fight the system and get out. He eventually gave up. I tried so hard to help him. My heart breaks at the thought of him and of all his losses. He had it more together than most who do not have a disability.

Society must focus on what we have to offer. Therapists need to help us do that.

I did not receive any help until the most painful parts of the illness were behind me. I suffered from tremendous loneliness, trying to make sense of it all on my own. It made me very angry. I was frightened to do it alone again and again.

I blamed myself for twenty years. I truly believed I was the cause of my family's pain. My parent's marriage suffered tremendously after my breakdown. My mother and father obviously disagreed about how to deal with me. My father still has not talked to me about my illness, and neither has my sister. I wonder how they deal with it and what they think of me. I watched my parents slowly tear each other apart, and I took the brunt of their anger.

Along with the unanswered questions, why I have an illness left me with feelings of complete and utter devastation. The illness erased years out of my memory, years I will never have again. If only someone had helped.

My dad helped me find a job as a secretary at the State House. I asked: "But what about my illness?" He told me no one would care. That was hard to grasp since I was told everyone would reject me if they found out. The most logical way to deal with it was to not tell anyone. Later I learned that there are good people out there who do care and who are special enough to overlook a disability if they love you enough.

My family and I did not tell anyone for a year. My dad thought that when it went away, it would save me all that baggage. Paranoid schizophrenia does not just disappear. I believed that my illness would go away if I fought hard enough. My second breakdown was devastating. I was just learning how to survive on my own; to be independent. My parents were aging, and I needed to take care of myself.

Stigma goes far beyond psychiatrists and therapists. I always want to have health and dental insurance. Being stuck on MassHealth is not a free ride, but it is essential to have good healthcare coverage.

I have learned a lot about the worst of people and how it affects me and my life and how I handle my affairs. I get deeply hurt because I can't understand how someone can continually lash out and somehow justify their cruelty.

Stigma from employees and co-workers is unbearable at times. I have been a victim of cruelty and abuse in the workplace several times. A former co-worker and I were sitting at the staff table, laughing and joking. She took it a little too far, saying my name then raising her hand and making stabbing movements accompanied by the sound effects from the movie **Psycho**. Even at companies and agencies that treat and advocate for the mentally ill, there is still discrimination. The employee can sense this in many ways. It is sad and extremely enraging because it can turn into a hostile workplace. Discrimination can be easily disguised. People can be subtle, and before you know it you are being taken advantage of.

Stigma in the workplace is unacceptable. People who live with serious mental illness need to work to gain confidence and to enhance their self-esteem. Finding the courage to go to work every day and put on a professional demeanor is exhausting. Sometimes even socializing or a trip to the library can bring on severe victimization, which further isolates us from society. Some people do not have the energy and stamina to deal with much. There is always the fear of failing over and over. We need help from all avenues to make employment a reality for people with severe mental illness.

I have worked with children many times. Once I worked as an assistant teacher. If my employer and my co-workers knew I was disabled, especially having schizoaffective disorder, I would never have been hired.

Most people who have a disability want to work and are realistic about how much they can handle. When they are given the chance to choose what job, what salary, and what hours to work, they usually meet those expectations. We work to succeed and have a sense of purpose, not to be belittled and harassed. We have skills to bring to the economy, and we have the potential to learn new ways of doing things. Many employers set low expectations. That is the wrong idea. Low expectations lead only to low self-esteem. I know; it has happened to me too many times.

Being a victim of stigma is being a victim of cruelty, abuse, and hate. Every mental health professional uses the you're-not-alone phrase. Try it. Feel the burden so heavy it makes you feel as though you have someone sitting on your back. I can literally feel the weight, and no, it is not an expression. Feel the burden of guilt that others put on you to make you believe you ruined their lives. Feel the burden of loneliness when the symptoms and stress of just walking out the door is a major accomplishment. Feel the burden of secrecy, having parts of your life that will never be talked about.

It is not a happy feeling when your friends tell you to wake up and smell the coffee before you even tell them what is bothering you. It is not a happy feeling when your friends look at your home and say: **What's your problem? You're rich; you do not know what it means to suffer.** Feeling like you have to explain your life away is not easy. Having a therapist who does not want you to talk about trauma from the past is devastating.

I have accomplished a lot in my lifetime, and I am still very young. No one knows just how much I have suffered or how good I feel at times. People automatically think I could never feel natural and wholesome. Well, I do. And yes, I live with a mental health disorder, but medication can work well. There are days that I feel confident and self-assured. I do not feel guilty because I can be productive or because I have different roles to play. My self-identity is not one of a paranoid schizophrenic but as a person first—a daughter, sister, aunt, and taxpayer. I contribute to my society, and I have many friends, quality relationships. I am a person living with a disability.

Even so there are times I would love to run away. If I could only get rid of the label that has been put on me. I have many crosses to bear, as my mother would say. I need more than a vacation. I need to be free from the oppression of stigma. Our society must be more tolerant, respectful, and compassionate toward the mentally ill. Most people don't know the damage of their strange stares and their laughter. Feeling shunned for only wanting to help, takes away who I am and enrages me.

Professionals need to take action and help dispel the universal stigma of mental illness. They need to speak to and for others who need it most. We need to have it straight and not be left feeling we are weak and inadequate.

Families who are dealing with a loved one who's had a psychotic episode need to be referred to mental health agencies. Every situation is unique, but there is help out there. No one should do it alone, the burden is too great, and so many questions need to be answered.

Society created stigma; people perpetuate stigma. We need to rid ourselves of hate as a society. Abraham Lincoln suffered from depression, and so did Emily Dickinson. There are many people who live with a psychiatric disorder in our society who function as parents and as leaders in our community. The fear is real to come out of the closet.

Life is difficult for everyone. To keep a disability a secret only adds to the stigma. You must learn a lot, fast. Hiding it is devastating. My parents and I agreed not to tell anyone, even our relatives.

When I talked on *Chronicle*, friends and acquaintances called saying how proud they were of me. One friend said she was in tears and that I did not lose their friendship; they just didn't know what to do. Stigma can hurt others by stopping them from reaching out to help. It is hard to know who to trust, but no one should live alone with the tragedy and pain of mental illness.

13

SWEET FREEDOM

*Oh in my reverence
the Divine one,
please relieve this
worried mind.
The clock is forever
striking the half-hour,
and sweet freedom
is clicking at my heels.
Past the time of
truth that I think
the moment is now
to pay thine tither
and banish these
memories that give
such a life unrest.*

—BONNIE TWOMEY

MY OUTLOOK ON LIFE CHANGED SO MUCH. At first it felt weird to be free. So many of my living years had been spent trying to block out or hide my feelings. *Chill out, go with the flow, live for now* became my way of life. My family life had confused and bewildered my reality for many years until I moved out. Even so, we shared so much time and happiness together. I considered us close-knit, and we enjoyed each other's company. With my new life I need to be more consistent and balance my energy, which always changes and needs a lot of adjusting.

Searching for new answers about my recovery put the pieces of the puzzle together. Reconstructing a life that has been lost, out of place, confused, and unorganized is about reconciliation and acceptance of what was, not what could have been. Accepting one's worst nightmare is not as bad as losing your life while living. Being mentally ill is being a prisoner in your own mind. Remission is like a parole, testing things out. Recovery is personal freedom, unique to every individual.

It has been years since *The Bonnie Tapes* were shown. I have finally gained some status and earned back some respect that I lost. I feel like I have a little bit of an edge. When it comes down to it, I can feel it. *The Bonnie Tapes* led to so many good things in my life. I learned to become independent. I always had a drive in me to succeed in whatever I did. I had the courage to stand on my own.

The years I thought I lost are back and reside in a special place in my heart. Someone once told me that you never really lose years; you just continue to grow. At the time I didn't believe him and could not imagine thinking otherwise. Now I believe him and thank him for telling me that we never stop living our lives, learning, and growing.

Layla married and has a beautiful home in Arlington. It's kind of fun living in the same town. We can joke about the local paper. She lives up the street. I love it. She is still one of my closest friends. I worked hard to keep it that way. When I am together with my family, we talk about the Cape and the boat and listen to my father brag about connections and luxuries he and his friends share together.

I have watched the way we interact over the years. I understand the roles we all play much better. I know I can't change anything. At least I have peace of mind knowing I can fall back on my own ways, not my old ways that made me feel so unloved. I can stand on my own because I spend less time with them. I appreciated the time I spent with them, and any hard feelings I had were left at my door.

Moving to Arlington gave me personal freedom to explore my life and myself. I had healthy dreams and ambitions I would never have achieved without public assistance. My confidence was at an all-time high; I was on my own and happy with my life and myself. I bought a convertible sports car, went on a diet, and joined a gym in the center of town. I was still trying to lose the Clozaril weight—nothing short of tough.

I guess the truth in life is that we really don't know what will happen, what we should do instead of not do. If we really knew what our life meant, then we would stop searching for something more. Looking into ourselves and learning who we are and finding out what kind of place we have in the world is okay. But there comes a time in everyone's life when we need to live, love, and be loved without hesitation. Time changes people into someone they never met. But love doesn't change.

My mom gave me a plaque that says: *Hope is the song in your heart that never stops singing*, which is so profound to me. I could never live without hope. Who can? When life is tough and throws you a curveball, you cannot give up hope. There is an ocean filled and a sky lined with it. Positive thinking is like having a chocolate sundae with a cherry on top. It helps you deal in a healthier, more reasonable way.

After I analyzed myself and life for years, to finally think and believe in the good ways of life has truly enabled me to manage my symptoms and my challenges.

14

2/21/99

I am so relaxed today. My levels of stress are minimal, which allows me to not focus on my life and what I need to do to take care of myself. I feel like everything is in place.

I enjoy life to its fullest today. You know, I didn't have a lot to think about this morning. My muses brought me back to relaxation, and I felt self-confident. The sun is shining, classical music is playing on my radio, and I feel alive and happy. Feelings of peace and freedom are reflected in my spirit. I feel liberated and more in touch with reality and myself. I feel more normal today, and I know I have done so much good work to analyze and to try to work out so much. Life is not easy, but small surprises bring on small miracles. Oh, to love life again to its fullest. For so many years I thought my inner spirit was totally destroyed. I fought to regain it, not knowing whether I could or not. My faith and hope led me to this day. It is a glorious day.

Because I have learned to be more self-reliant, I do not feel like I have to shout to the world how I feel. I can be at peace with myself, knowing who I am and accepting all parts of me that go with it. I know it can be rough, and I know what I go through. What I also know is that I can keep my happiness along with it.

It feels weird to judge myself harshly. It is a major accomplishment for me to stop analyzing parts of my life that I don't have to. Worrying about unnecessary parts of my life is replaced with vitality. I refuse to be a martyr. I have a disability, but I will not self-loathe or let darkness enter into my spirit when I feel healthy. When you feel good, you feel good. Why make yourself miserable or feel guilty about it?

My illness and life seem to go in endless circles, like a tornado. I move on, learning new lessons in life every time. Yes, repairing a life that is destroyed is scary and unpredictable. I guess my friends were justified in giving me the nickname Hurricane Bonnie.

One morning I began thinking about my mom. She sacrificed her happiness to stay in her marriage and sacrificed so much within her marriage to keep me home, preventing me from experiencing a painful life of halfway houses and hospitals I could never have completely recovered from. I am so thankful to her for giving me a chance. She was always the buffer between my dad and me. She always stuck up for me. I was completely unaware that she was doing this, so I was shocked and surprised to hear her tell me they would argue about me, still.

My mom was a source of fun and laughter for many. Some of my friends have told me that she would single them out from a crowd and somehow make them feel special. My relationship with my mom was more complicated. She knew much more about me than my dad or Layla. We experienced many difficult times and many happy moments together. She worried about me and how I would survive on my own, knowing that my dad and sister were not sensitive to any of my needs, which included accepting my disability and helping me manage. It was all on my mother's shoulders.

While I was living in my apartment in Arlington, she would come to me in a panic, telling me how much she needed to get away from my dad. She was going to leave him and rent an apartment, which she thought he would pay for. But my father would never help her out financially. He treated her like dirt. He wouldn't give her enough money for grocery shopping and complained when she asked for more. She was unable to work and so depressed. She would ask me for money. It was awful. I felt horrid when I told her I didn't have any money.

She never knew my social personality or how I interacted with others beyond family and family friends. At home I was one person. The minute I passed my driveway, I was someone else. How I separated this was beyond me; I just wish I could have shown them who I really was. When I was happy around her, it felt natural; she thought I was high or manic. *No, Bonnie could never feel good about herself.* I can't help sense that the quality of my relationships were underestimated and under-valued because they never met most of my friends nor did they ever ask me about them.

She loved her grandchildren as if they were her own. My mom would be at her sewing machine for hours, making the kids new clothes. A lot of care and hard work went into it. She quilted blankets and gave them as gifts to many people she loved. A day never goes by that I don't remember her and how thoughtful she was.

She was a strong woman, but it hurt her more to hide her pain and push everything under the rug. She remained dedicated to her husband as much as she could for as long as she could. My mom tried to uphold the family name for my dad, but she became visibly more upset, angry, and hurt in the end.

My mom had a relapse with her cancer, and I struggled to keep my life together. I was attending graduate school at

Boston University at the time. I received a full scholarship to their prestigious psychiatric rehabilitation program, one of the best in the country. My family didn't show much support. My mom sent me a card of congratulations. I did very well. I was offered an internship as a mentor/tutor at a local mental health agency. I loved the job and my clients. But I couldn't keep up with the demands and lost the internship and ultimately my scholarship. I never went back to that field again. I also lost my relationships but kept my apartment.

Her last hope to beat the cancer was to try an experimental chemotherapy. The first day of the trial, Layla drove my mother and me to Dana Farber. She dropped us off at the front door then left with her kids to go to the beach. For one of her tests I had a plain view of her heart monitor. The clinicians drew blood, mixed it with an agent, then injected it back into her bloodstream to make sure the chemicals in the chemo didn't kill her. She was very, very brave.

After the initial tests were completed, we went to the infusion room. The doctors went over the risks—the worst-case scenario was the treatment could be fatal—and told her that the first ten minutes of the chemo were crucial. There were three IV bags. I held her hand as the orange-red substance flowed slowly down the line and into her vein. She did remarkably but was unraveled and fatigued by the end of the day and wanted to go home, but Layla was very late picking us up.

After we finally made it back to Mom's house, I stayed with her all day and night until my dad came home. He didn't call or leave any messages, showing up about 11:30 drunk with a big, "Hi. How was everyone's day?"

I asked where he'd been, and he said a political fundraiser. The tension between my parents was alarming. I asked Mom if she wanted me to stay, so she wouldn't be alone with him. She said no. I went home but came back to the house early the next morning. My mother was beside herself. She could not stand still and kept saying she had to get out of there and was leaving for the Cape. I convinced her to let me take her, so we left for a few days. She was engaging in tasks she should not have been. I talked with her, but she was angry and anticipating the rest of the family coming down.

Layla and my father pulled up exuding a *Who gives a shit?* attitude. My mom called me into the house and told me to tell Layla to do her own laundry, cooking, and running of the house. Layla was spread out on a lawn chair with an ugly, unrecognizable expression, and I related what Mom said. She didn't look at me or say anything.

My mom begged me to stay, but I had to work. As I pulled away, I saw her look at me with a longing I'll never forget.

My last memory is driving to the end of our street. The next moment it's dark, and I'm sitting on my couch in my apartment in Arlington, contemplating suicide. I took enough pills to put me out for days. My mom visited, which I don't remember. When I regained complete consciousness, I made the decision not to hide my pain, my attempt to commit suicide. Ultimately, I lost my scholarship because I couldn't keep my responsibilities at work to the high standards expected of me.

I was angry with the school for letting me go so easily. I was angry at the mental health field for not being there for me.

I moved to Burlington, and everything stopped. The calls to speak or lecture, to run a group, to speak on a panel or local television show. There was not much in my life after that.

Layla took over my mother's care without consulting me. She took her to chemo sessions and doctor appointments. I wasn't told when the appointment was. I don't know whose idea it was. I regretfully stayed away but called her every day.

It was difficult to stand up to Layla. She would call my father, and he would call me, taking away my rights to go to the Cape alone, for example. My mother worried about me having my father and Layla left to take care of me. She was in a panic and went to therapy.

She had liposarcoma, cancer of the fatty tissue. There was no known treatment back then because her cancer was so rare. The team at Dana-Farber developed an experimental chemo never used for treatment before. She developed breast cancer but had to postpone treatment because the liposarcoma took precedence. Diabetes lurked too, and she had an awful time trying to inject herself with insulin. She couldn't work. I can't imagine how frightened and alone she must have felt.

My mom passed away from cancer the day after my forty-first birthday. She took all the answers with her. After ten long years of fighting the battle, she was taken away after complications from her surgery. She spent a year going between the hospital and the rehabilitation center. She was on a rollercoaster of making progress and deterioration. Mom came home for several weeks once in a while, but she ended up back in the hospital every time.

Mom called me several weeks before she died. Her voice was strong and alert.

"Hi," she said. "I'm coming home!"

I was so happy to hear from her. It was the last time I ever held a conversation with her.

When she died, I lived in Burlington, a few towns away from my dad's home. A part of me died with her. Everything was different. She brought our family and friends together, especially on holidays. After she died no one came around on Christmas Eve. We always had a nice gathering to celebrate together. We didn't know how to cook a turkey!

I felt the changes years ago when Mom started her chemo.

I lost everything, even my sleep. I needed a whole new way of coping. I risked losing everything because I lost my support system and felt I had no one to rely on for my needs but myself. Her death has saddened me since. I would visit her grave, set out a lawn chair, and read a book and sit with her.

I continued to make friendships after the hardest part of my grief had settled. A friend I knew from my residential counselor days offered me the opportunity to be a counselor at a duel diagnosis residence, teaching the clients about recovery. It was there where I met May, who became one of my best friends. She was a wonderful friend, always there for me and always accepted me and understood me.

I tried to forgive my mother for all the hurt in our relationship before her passing, but it was tough. I tried to love her and care for her, but she would be deceptive and not let me in after the first session. When I tried to help her, she would manipulate her schedule so that it was impossible for me to be with her. It tore me apart. After a while I gave up offering to help; it hurt too much to be shunned. She only let my sister Layla play a major role in transporting her to the hospital for chemo treatments. The only way I could communicate with her was to call her every morning without fail.

I miss her. It is difficult depending only on myself, especially with all the love loss in my family. But I still appreciate that those of us left still get together on special occasions. The lack of communication is painful. What does remain constant is my unending love for my family, regardless of how they feel for me. Layla has shown she cares at times. When my life was empty with not many friends, she included me in Thursday movie nights with the girls. But they didn't even look at me, so eventually I stopped going.

I have healed tremendously from the suffering I endured. It has taken a lot of time and energy to accept that there are things I can't change. I realized everyone has limitations, and I needed to understand that receiving love and acceptance can be conditional. Knowing that I can't change other people has been a drain on my self-esteem and an actual turning point. I needed to believe the only person I can change is me. My TEC song reflected that to make changes in the world, you need to start with yourself.

My mom was a great friend and one of the greatest people I ever met. She taught me how to set the table and be gracious. My mom taught me how to dress appropriately for every occasion—shabby wasn't in her vocabulary. I always had to look my best. She never complained and was extremely modest. She lived without a car until I was in college. Her strength and unconditional love of God, hope, and goodness in the world nurtured a sense of acceptance and an example for me to be genuine and honest.

There were times when I felt as though everyone had abandoned me, but my mom was by my side with a cup of coffee and a handful of tissues. She taught me to be open and to express my feelings naturally. When I would get off track and cop an attitude, she would disapprove. But she was always right. Because of my desire to please her, I lived by her example. She helped me keep both feet on the ground and not get caught up in myself.

I loved to sit on her bed and talk about everything. Sometimes we would read together. We played cards and oh, did we have fun. Every time we played, we would break into spontaneous laughter. She had a great sense of humor and loved to pull pranks on my dad. She loved to party. She was so blessed and did not know it. If she only knew how many people loved her. Who do I turn to when I want to share part of my life? She helped me figure things out and listened endlessly. My mom had so much hope in her heart. I truly believe she nurtured that hope in my heart as well.

AFTER MY MOTHER'S DEATH I needed major shoulder surgery when I was forty-eight years old. I had chronic pain, and physical therapy didn't work. I found out I have osteo-arthritis and had fractured it in five places from the wear and tear. Layla had me live with her for about a week. She took good care of me. I don't remember most of it except I had to sit up 24/7. I could never get comfortable, which I complained about insistently. My exercise sessions at the gym were cancelled, and I gained too much weight. I endured painful physical therapy for four months. It took over twelve months to recover. I called my therapist the Terminator. The range of motion never completely returned, making some everyday tasks difficult or impossible. My shoulder is in constant pain, especially when I stretch it or lay on it. I can't hold heavy objects.

I continued to feel the need to take care of myself the best I could. I had so many different kinds of pain killers I recognized the need to get off them. So, I went to the medicine cabinet and gave it a clean sweep and dumped all the drugs into the trash. To drive ten minutes up the highway was a challenge. But after time and careful practice, I was able to get back on the road again.

Some months later I realized I hadn't had a mammogram

for more than three years, so I scheduled an exam. After the exam I had an ultrasound that detected a mass in each breast. I kept it together and called my sister. She was a great support.

I scheduled biopsies, which were brutal. I laid facedown on a table designed for two breasts to come out two holes. The doctor used somewhat of a gun device because it made a loud clicking sound, to take samples of tissue. Another woman was present to hold me down to make sure I didn't move. The procedure was painful, even with a local anesthetic, and the doctor complained I shouldn't be in that much discomfort.

After the biopsy I lay on a metal hospital table and waited alone to get the results. Two unfamiliar doctors dressed in long white coats entered the room.

One of the doctors told me, "We think it's cancer."

Hearing that, I felt all the blood flow out of my face. I was in shock. This was the worst news I ever heard. With horror I followed the doctor's directions and scheduled all the procedures to prepare for surgery as recommended.

God put the strength in me to fight cancer. I had no time to sit, worry, and cry. I canceled my apartment move and quit cigarettes. I shopped for personal needs and food. I pulled everything together myself and never complained.

My sister Layla and I waited in the exam room at the oncology department for the results. He told me I had cancer. I looked at Layla and noticed she was trying to hold back her tears. He talked about a lumpectomy and radiation. I thought I should have no radiation treatments. He disagreed.

An upper body mold was made so I would be lined up perfectly. My arms needed to be raised over my head for forty-five minutes at a time to make the mold. It was extremely painful on my bad arm, so I took a painkiller before each session.

I had two lumpectomies within two weeks because the surgeon misjudged the borders. I underwent eight consecutive weeks of radiation. It burned my skin so badly I ended up with a large sore underneath my arm and suffered from radiation fatigue. The level of exhaustion was disabling. It burned inside. I would shop for two or three hours and then be in bed for days. It took several years for the fatigue to stabilize or be the same constantly. No one understood it or why I couldn't hold a commitment. I gave it all I had, but there were times I hated myself for doing so little.

A month or two after my cancer diagnosis, I was diagnosed with heart disease: left ventricle hypertrophic cardiomyopathy. I was told by my cardiologist that it's inherited, and there was nothing I could do about it. After a cardiac episode caused me to collapse and end up hospitalized, I was taken off two major psych meds that doctors worried could be dangerous, possibly fatal, with my heart disease. Neither drug was ever replaced. My sister and my dad were not there for me. I needed them to get me on a medication regimen to keep me stable. They showed no caring or support, so I suffered tremendously and needlessly for three years. I didn't know my sister was dealing with my father's bad health. I believe she was expected to take care of him, and I was put aside and had to take care of myself.

I was under more stress and pressure to keep my life together. My landlord tried to put me in a studio, but I refused. I held it up, held it in, and slipped it out until my mind screamed louder than anyone should have heard. Smoking that cigarette I shouldn't have, I contemplated going to that crazy hospital I detest even the sound of.

Several months after my heart diagnosis, I felt as though I had penetrated a deep, human darkness to a pain I never knew to exist. There was no choice for me but to take the one chance I had left. For once the universe didn't listen to me; it exiled me and tormented my very being. I no longer existed to my family, friends, and community. *Why is this happening to me?*

Carl Jung claimed he ran into many "spontaneous, meaningful coincidences of so high a degree of improbability as to appear flatly unbelievable."

My life was a perfect storm, so I rode it until the very end. I can't speak about it in a few sentences, nor will everybody believe what I say. It was tightly woven in deceit and lies, and because of this, all the truths can never be told. Everything in my life was manageable until they started to discontinue my psychiatric medications.

I accepted my unpredictable reality and fought for someone, something I truly believed in. My heart disease diagnosis meant the possibility of sudden death. I was so lost and frightened. My psych meds still needed to be adjusted because I continued to have mental health issues.

Part of dealing with cancer and heart disease was that I needed to quit cigarette smoking. Laura, an old friend who had stage-three breast cancer, was a huge support. She emphasized I needed to quit because I wouldn't want to admit to my oncologist I still smoked during every office visit. I did quit and was proud of my accomplishment.

Other old girlfriends turned away. May had hip surgery at the same time I was treated for breast cancer. We tried so hard to keep our relationship healthy because we'd known each other for years and were each other's cheerleader. My aunt, who I thought cared for me a great deal, turned her back when I told her I had breast cancer.

She said, "I don't have space in my head for you."

She never called me again until two years later. No one did. So I grew sicker and sicker until I fell silent, almost completely mute. Neither my aunt nor Layla told anyone about my cancer. It was a grave mistake for me not to reach out to any other family members I felt close to. My aunt Sally was there for me every day, but I still felt heartbroken and alone. I felt abandoned after those close to me, who I thought would reach out, never did. I was sick and confused and considered the rest of my family, such as my cousins who lived nearby, to be my cavalry, but they never came to save me from all the madness. I thought this because I was sick with mental health problems. I thought everyone knew but didn't care to contact me, but they never knew.

Although I suffered from emotional struggles, I changed after cancer. I was a strong woman to get through it, but I needed to build relationships with other women who had suffered from breast cancer. My belief in Jesus, in God, placed a remarkable strength in my core. I remember sitting waiting for radiation, wondering how I was sitting so still, focused, and clear.

Dan lived in apartment 68C. Mine was 68D right next door. He answered my ad posted on the hallway bulletin board. He shoveled me out all winter for $20.00 a storm. I apologized for not giving him more; I was embarrassed I couldn't afford any more than that. He didn't mind. I thought about his appreciation for so little, which I would have loved to understand. I was attracted to his complete sincerity.

We grew an attraction to each other the summer of my battle with cancer. We talked on the wall of our apartment complex grounds for hours and laughed until our bellies hurt. Neighbors would pass us by with a wave and a smile. People passed by us in their cars and beeped their horns or waved and smiled at us. Everything was perfect. My trials seemed lighter, even though the burden was heavy. I wanted to know every detail about his life, work, friends, and where he'd lived. I loved telling him too much. I mentioned I had watched a trial my father prosecuted as assistant attorney general around 1977. He knew about it! I knew it was a famous case, but I was still shocked.

I learned about the motorcycle accident that changed the

course of his life on September 16, 2012. He broke his ankle and became permanently disabled after having a bad surgery. He could not work, lost his apartment, and he moved in with his mother next door to me. He applied for disability and was waiting for the decision. My birthday is September 16, 1964. We were both born in 1964. The similarity of these dates enthralled me because I knew there had to be a reason why. He had the best personality and was patient, kind, and smart. To me he was always the coolest man in the world. And I fell in love with him.

When we became restless we took local road trips or drove to New Hampshire. Still affected by the radiation fatigue I was too exhausted to drive more than half an hour and would pull over when I felt lightheaded. We did nice things together like walk along the Medford reservoir or go to the lake in Woburn. We never had a loss for words. We shared a quality of life together that was easy, undemanding.

I found out he smoked pot. I didn't like the idea, so he would not get high around me. I did try it, and all I did was laugh about everything. I couldn't stop. So, I never tried it again.

Early one morning while Dan was still asleep, I collapsed to the ground one morning while taking a walk. I crawled home and called a taxi to take me to the emergency room. I was told I was lucky to be there because my heart rhythm could have been fatal. I was admitted for observation. Consulting doctors decided that I wear a portable monitor for two weeks. They discontinued two major psych meds at once and didn't replace them. They thought they were the catalyst and could have resulted in death. I couldn't deal with life without the medication, and it took a toll on me.

I quickly became delusional. My thoughts were paranoid and grandiose. I felt terrorized each day. I thought I was a pawn between my father and Dan's mother's boyfriend. Why and for what I had no clue—maybe drugs. My cousin Katie invited my dad and me to lunch at a popular restaurant in Winchester. Katie and her two boys were celebrating their high school graduation. My father glared at me throughout the entire meal. I have never seen him so hateful. I thought he'd heard the rumors on the street about me being a pawn. I didn't know what more to make out of it.

They couldn't get me to listen. The rumors terrorized me, and I felt like an awful person who couldn't defend herself and say: *No, I didn't do anything wrong.* My delusions were torture. Sometimes I completely believed everything I experienced was real—the hate, the fear of being killed, and of being tracked. But it wasn't, and I had no help.

I didn't give up. I had nothing to hold on to, so I fought to stay with Dan.

I walked into a Staples, and everyone looked at me and stopped whatever they were doing. The store fell silent. I believed then most of what I had been experiencing was real. I needed medication to sort it all out, but my doctor refused to help despite my pleading for care. I asked her to refer me to a group. She told me I knew what I was going through and discontinued two more medications. She should have been held accountable. My life fell apart pretty quickly, and my mind went crazy. I don't know if there is a human word to describe the unrelenting horror, confusion, and anger I experienced. I believed a rumor started that I was a crack whore out of control. I thought I was vulnerable to negotiations. Again, I perceived it as real from strangers. How could I not believe it? I was confused, not knowing why this was happening and why no one asked if any of these awful things really happened to me.

I felt overwhelmed, drifty, and completely engrossed in depression. I lost respect for myself. I was at the lowest point in my life and considered committing suicide. I didn't, and decided to fight for some sort of reality.

My paranoia and grandiose thoughts made my feelings

and emotions seem enlarged. I envisioned a huge, black mass always at my back. Though I'd grown stronger through my experiences with cancer, I needed more help than what I received. I accepted there was no way I could control my future. I spent a year believing I would be killed every time I left my apartment because everyone hated me. I gave up any hope of having a better life and thought I had to leave Dan because I needed to battle my mental illness.

16

MY FATHER CONTINUED HIS JOURNEY of hate and abuse by telling me to go back to my club. I asked Dan what he meant by that; he said he didn't know. At the time I had no idea my dad was suffering from lung and pancreatic cancer. When I told him I was going to the General Hospital to have a heart monitor placed in me he told me he had cancer. His eyes glazed over like he was numb.

I wasn't included when it came to his treatments. I called the hospital every week to find out when my father's appointment was with his oncologist. The day of his appointments he would not look at me, nor would he sit with me in the waiting room. I didn't know what I had done wrong. I felt like the worst person in the world.

He was in hospice until his death. My dad looked lifeless—no IVs and he wasn't eating. His mouth was open, his eyes were cloudy, and his pupils were constricted.

I included myself in one of his chemo sessions but was kicked out because the nurse told Layla having the both of us there were too many people.

About two months before he died, Layla loaded a dump truck with all his belonging and posted a picture on Facebook of her smiling in a dump truck holding a campaign sign with *Twomey* written in bold letters, like she had won a prize.

The way my father and Layla had treated me before he died eventually put me over the edge, especially with my psych meds not being replaced. I told her none of this would have happened with early intervention, taking care of my mental health.

When my dad passed away, somehow all the money from the assets disappeared. I never knew what was said about me. My attorney told me he had my back. His law firm had my life in their hands, and my financial advisor, Robert, who I met through my attorney, supported me through the probate battle.

I remember sitting in my car at the lake, terrified that strange men were looking at me because they were heroin dealers and would hurt me. I thought I had to notice everything around me to protect myself from others hurting me. There was a white SUV on my right, and the man got in the driver's seat without noticing. It shook me up a little too much. Then a young man was sitting on the curb to my left. I thought I was in the middle of something going down really bad and needed to leave. By the time I got home, I was so paranoid I parked in the lot farthest from my building. The radio was telling me how to move my body and let me know what was going on and when I could go home.

When I did finally get home that night, I had a severe loss of stability. I slipped rather quick, hard and deep. I broke into a million pieces. I complained to my landlord that my neighbors downstairs had a knife. I showed some concern but then quickly left the office. Then I called the police to complain about the noise they were making.

I thought drugs were put in my food so I rummaged through everything without my intention being completely pointless. The police came. There were three of them. I remember the police asking if Dan abused me. I have no memory of what I said about him or why. An officer asked me if he could talk with someone else who knew him. I gave him the number of an aunt. He called her and she told him she didn't know anything about Dan but that my heart monitor should be a concern. Because of this, an ambulance came and I was brought to the emergency room.

I remember being put in the middle of the reception area on a stretcher. I was frantic not knowing what was happening to me. A young staff member came up to me and told me that I was in a lot of trouble. Finally, I was put in a room but with a security guard in front of my door. I was frantic! Asking myself what did I do, is everyone in my building arrested, how is Dan, did they arrest him too? I could not use the restroom without a security guard and a staff member outside my door. I left my room to ask someone a question about my status and a nurse towered over me and shouted for me to go to my room. She held her arm out above me and pointed to where I was placed. I cowered away from her along with any dignity I ever had. The confusion and madness plagued me like nothing else did.

I hadn't eaten in days and they did not give me my medication. I was extremely weak and vulnerable because I had no advocate, no one was watching out for me.

At least four physicians pressured me to decide whether or not I wanted to sign a voluntary commitment order or a partial hospitalization. I didn't sign anything and I wanted to talk to my doctor first. She never showed up. I had no idea what was happening and no way to protect myself.

It was 4:00 a.m. and I left the ER under orders I was no threat to myself or others, and that I was a low hospital risk. Also in my medical records it stated two blood tests were drawn and showed no substance abuse.

I was transferred to another ambulance. The EMT who rode with me in the back snickered and told me I would get out. The winter sun was rising and after what seemed a long ride, we pulled up to a small building. I had no idea where I was. I was in horror.

I waited in an empty hall and reception room. Finally, I was called in to a room where I surrendered all my belongings including my heart monitor. I was strip searched, put in a johnny and photographed. I was then led to a gymnasium and sat in the middle of a basketball court where half a dozen young men were playing. Pleading to get something to eat and sleep I was told to wait another hour until the group was over. I was ready to pass out. We left the court and went through several metal doors that gave out a loud buzz to be opened.

The first person I met told me, "You have a very short memory." She then asked what am I like when I am stressed. I didn't know what to say so I said I fidgeted. I was shown a room devoid of any belongings except a single, unfitted sheet, a white summer blanket and a pillow. I felt my mind go blank, seeing nothing but static.

I had only the clothes on my back so I wore them the full four days I was there. They confiscated my phone, heart monitor, and everything in my pocketbook. They would not let me use the one phone bolted to the cement wall. I told them I needed to work out the final details to my apartment move. I was scheduled to move in less than one week. I was not allowed to make any calls. My cat was very sick. I wanted to keep her home as long as I could until she was ready to pass away. I was able to have someone check in on her but no one did. I never knew where I was. No one ever told me.

It was horrifying to hear Dan outside my window every night being hauled off by the police. It was all acted out like a play about three times over. I would hear him scream and I would cry so hard, but quietly so no one would hear me.

I was put on suicide check every five minutes. When I spent social time with the six men who were patients there a staff member would observe me in less than 30 seconds and check something off on a clipboard.

The windows were frosted and barred by thick metal. It was winter and I was cold. The blanket in my room was the only thing I had to keep me warm but staff told me I couldn't use it. One of the men, a patient there, lent me his sweater.

Most of the time when I asked someone behind the desk for something they would turn and walk away. Everything was scheduled. Even for water. They took away all cups and crackers after dinner in the cafeteria.

There were three groups a day. One particular session emphasized the next time any one of us returned we would be a statistic, which we would not want.

I never saw a physician, only to be told I needed to stay a fourth day. When that came up my discharge papers looked like a grammar school piece of paper written about the two levels of stress. A social worker signed along with my signature.

I had no money, but was told a van would give me a ride home and would take a credit card. They didn't. I went into a convenience store where the ATM didn't work and the clerk wouldn't look at me. Miraculously, after four times it spat out $40 for my ride home.

When I finally arrived, I found a notice taped to my door. It was a demand to leave the premise because I terminated my lease and the new tenants were scheduled to move in and I had not moved out yet. My new landlord was furious because I had not finalized the paperwork for me to move in and she had prospective tenants that could rent the apartment. Talking with my new landlord did not go well. She was extremely angry and didn't understand why I couldn't call her. I told her I was in the hospital and had no way of contacting her. Needless to say I lost my new apartment. My landlord made an agreement with me to stay at my old apartment.

The staff at the hospital gave me a one-month supply of medication with no refills. They told me to call an agency at 9:00 a.m. when I got home to get a new prescriber. I called at 9:05 the next morning and they berated me and told me to call the next morning at 9:00.

I was frantically making calls to new insurance companies. I was treated very badly and was not able to secure new health care. Finally, as a last resort I called an old insurer and gained insurance where I could stay away from that ER.

I found myself in real fear of being left. I was terrified to live alone. Dan was not going to move in with me to the new apartment. He told me I would find out what was real and what was not. After what happened he stayed with me through my trauma and newly developed PTSD.

About eight months later Dan and I moved to Gloucester. We needed each other more now than ever.

He learned he didn't have a job down our street at a convenience store after they initially told him he did. We thought we were okay. Devastated, he applied to every store he could find with no luck. Our relationship was tested to such limits we didn't sleep together in the same bed. Eventually, he left because I couldn't support him on my Trust and my credit cards were maxed out. Robert and my landlord forced him out because he couldn't pay rent and wouldn't leave on his own. I worried about him and felt enormous guilt and sadness. I needed him so much and missed him terribly. We lost all contact after that.

Losing everything, Dan, my family, friends, health insurance, apartment, my peace of mind, somehow, with the Grace of God, I was able to struggle through the deep cuts of trauma and mental illness and stand on my two feet and say, "I have this."

I knew how to take care of myself through my experience of having mental illness. I learned what worked and what didn't. I kept focused on what felt real and balanced. I knew this was my last chance because of the enormity of my burden. I had to fight for my life, my dignity, and most of my ability to love life and people. It takes so much energy to move on and to do it over again. I needed to put all my survival skills in place so that I would have something to fall back on.

I look for words to tell how I get through every day, even a bad day. I thought to myself I want to get rid of my pain so I try to do things better and achieve more mostly on a bigger scale. Sometimes I pull out the Ajax and clean.

The things I had to do to find my balance were simple. But to dig through all the rubble to find simplicity was near impossible. So, some parts of my life will never be rescued, not there to be real. Others flourished like buds on a tree in the springtime.

Not long after Dan left I was diagnosed with COPD. Shortly after that I was diagnosed with kidney disease. I slowly brought some family in my life and was careful not to overwhelm them with information but nurtured each relationship with trust.

I began counseling once a week for several years. I wanted to sue the institutions who hurt me but Robert and my therapist told me not to because it was too much money and it would cause me too much anger. My therapist had a written request for my medical records sent to both the ER and the lockdown facility. Both institutions denied I was a patient there. So, I let it go and started a new life. As a result of painfully losing everything I knew or cared about I did not trust anyone, became vigilant, and kept my eyes open to stay away from trouble and others who could get me in trouble. I was alone, missing my mother, hearing her calling me on a tearful night. Layla's voice would tell me I wasn't okay.

I was presented with decisions whether or not to keep either my mental or physical health due to complications with my psychiatric medications and heart and kidney disease. I had to discontinue my Lithium because it wore down my kidneys. A new medication replaced it but slowed me down and my meds made it almost impossible to think.

I was completely frightened and saddened and prayed every night. I would have done so many things differently. Mostly showing how much I loved everyone by bringing them into my life when I needed them with no complaining or shedding fear to have them listen to my pain. I would have sought out friendships rather than be determined to deal on my own. My isolation became a way of life that its energy seeped from me, having no love or companionship. Living with this sadness I was able to find my way to live some sort of whole again, but with accepting a very unhealthy, threatening state of being. For all the people I kept so far from me, my heart came home to open up and accept them as they are, when they are hurtful and when they are kind. To put aside my problems, to love life and people again and to appreciate what I had, not what I didn't have, is a joy. My faith brought on a new meaning of leaning on the things that bring me life and to be open to what changes will come in the unpredictable future. No matter what the challenges, and for all the tearful nights and hopeful mornings, I will survive and enjoy another day.

JOY IS MY GUIDE TO WHOLENESS, not sadness. My sense of fulfillment is being strong and having the courage to face the daily pain. I know to take the risk to not fear tomorrow or the next moment. The purest loss I have experienced I will not let go of because it is that loss that made me full, love.

I won't spend the rest of my life trying to unlearn my mistakes. It's too late for that. I felt enormous outrage and I needed to cry every night before I went to sleep. My sadness was deep, and I grieved at the loss of my father.

My sense of abandonment and aloneness was profound. I began to find my peace in about six months. Willing and enthusiastic about starting a new life, I burst out and joined groups and volunteered at one-day jobs at the YMCA and took courses at a local writers' club. It was difficult to function and learn how to get through at first. But I hung in and fought, and slowly my activities became easier to manage when I participated. When I wasn't volunteering, I slept for a year. I was just so tired.

How many times am I going to let someone hurt me and take advantage of me before I let go of that person and search for someone better? How much am I willing to sacrifice without being judged, misunderstood, or receiving love back? I need that person who I think will only know me in my fullest and not stunt my personal growth and every area of my life. I let them take complete control over me and make me feel like there is something wrong with me.

Who am I now? I thought if I could fill my calendar and keep my commitments, I would somehow emerge as whole. I was very wrong. I am empty. I lost everything I loved, sacred and dear. So who am I now? An empty, oversized container that had aged twenty years in two months. I felt like crap.

I realized I needed to smile and say hello to my neighbors. I did and got a nice and happy: *Hello; how are you?* in return. It was then I realized if I continued to walk around unwanted, I would be unwanted.

I opened up my heart and my mind to possibilities that will be fortunate and happy. That dark place is visited by me less and less each day. Some days are hard. I sent Robert my WRAP wellness plan, a guide to how I would like my treatment and care to be given. He lived with me through some of the darkest times of my life. He and my attorney are working hard on finding me homeownership. No one in their right mind would criticize these two men. They are my rocks.

The fact is, when the battle is over, you count what you have left. For me, no matter how much hate I had for my sister, I was thankful my attorneys did not harm her. I had that. I kept my dignity and didn't call anyone in my family or our friends to complain. I let the chips fall, and they did. Who won the battle? My sister because she was in control and got all the money. Who won the fight? Many parts of it, I did. Now the rest is to lead a good life. I was always told by my dad that the Twomey's are fighters. My dad taught me how to protect myself: always keep my guard up and never let the bastards get you down. I was angry that I let myself lose my family and friends. Lesson learned.

When I was young I thought I could take on the world. I chose to enhance my life by creating positive self-images with each role and learning from them. With my faith I learned what to change and what not to change. I put down my pride and released my anger. This guided me through my hardships and brought me closer to my truer self.

I have a passion for helping others and for being around people I like. Relationships are complicated in any circumstance. Having a disability, it is a great accomplishment to discover myself in a relationship in which I am treated with respect and genuine kindness.

I have to watch out for triggers. It may be negative thinking or taking on something new. When I feel overwhelmed I have to take it easy on myself, relax, and appreciate what I have in my life. My coping skills become more focused when I redirect my energies by setting realistic goals.

I have been afraid to live alone but learned an invaluable lesson. I should have reached out. I am not alone. I decided to contact my family, aunts and cousins. They were all happy to hear from me, and some extended an invitation to get together. They never stopped loving me. I was a very sick woman and left them when I most needed help. In hindsight I wish I had reached out before my life became unmanageable.

Many of us need to leave the life we have known and go on path B, whether it is to move on from old hurts, addictions, abuse, or failing health. Even a mental illness requires a great deal of skill learning to cope and have a decent life. I learned I can always take better care of myself than anyone else could.

I like to give people the benefit of the doubt and see the best in them. I associated myself with people who were homeless at one point in their life, and scholars writing books, teaching, and running the state. The difference in social standing didn't matter to me because they were all real with a story waiting to be told. Being judged wrong by so many people, it was difficult to find out who I was. I refused to judge anyone else because I thought it would be cruel to have someone search for themselves out of thoughtlessness. I learned to respect all kinds of people from different demographics and ethnic backgrounds. A few of the people who had the most influence on me as an adult have been addicts or homeless at one point in their lives.

My life was built around my mother, father, and older sister. My mom died an undignified death and my dad died in a rage at me. I wish Layla could share this beautiful and painful time in my life. Maybe she would learn I am a real person, not a joke. I reached out to her three times, but she didn't respond. I want to forgive her. My peace lay in letting people go where and when they may.

I won't give up on myself, and will continue to work toward not feeling helpless or powerless. I live every day like it is my last without the tremendous fear of death, because that makes living fully humanly impossible. Realizing I am brave enough to trust what I see around me keeps me independent and adequate enough to stay out of the hospital and to survive in society.

After moving to Gloucester and getting good health care, I was put back on a medication regimen that works. Because of that I was able to take care of my physical problems, including heart and kidney disease. After many years of poor health I opened up my heart again; and my spirit came home. I chose not to be only an observer of my own life but to learn how to manage the difference between a bad day and a good day even when feeling like crap.

On my endless path of recovery, I will continue to stop reacting on emotional impulses and not react until I think it through. *Is it really what it seems, and could that happen? Would someone really do that? What are other explanations? Do I reach out? Who can I trust and not be annoying? How do other people react to the same situation?*

I have established healthy relationships with my aunt Lois and my aunt Valerie. It takes trust and work. My aunt Lois showed me she loves me unconditionally. My aunt Val got me through some of the hardest most lonely holiday seasons I ever had, celebrating alone. I nurture these relationships and treasure them.

ABOUT THE AUTHOR

BONNIE TWOMEY is currently pursuing her interest in painting and abstract art. She volunteered at a local art gallery pre-Covid 19. Her work was accepted into a juried art exhibit in Gloucester. She also remains a mental health advocate, committed to helping people manage their mental illness so they can achieve their full potential.

Sweet Freedom

Mending a Heart Broken by Mental Illness

Bonnie Twomey

Author website: BonnieTwomey.com

Publisher: SDP Publishing

Also available in ebook format

SDP Publishing

www.SDPPublishing.com

Contact us at: info@SDPPublishing.com

CPSIA information can be obtained
at www.ICGtesting.com
Printed in the USA
FSHW020611091120
75595FS